# SUPER
# SALADS

# GOOD HOUSEKEEPING

# SUPER
# SALADS

## 70 FRESH AND SIMPLE RECIPES

★ GOOD FOOD GUARANTEED ★

HEARST
books

**HEARST**BOOKS

An Imprint of Sterling Publishing Co., Inc.
1166 Avenue of the Americas
New York, NY 10036

ISBN 978-1-61837-296-3

The Good Housekeeping Cookbook Seal guarantees that the recipes in this publication
meet the strict standards of the Good Housekeeping Institute. The Institute has been a
source of reliable information and a consumer advocate since 1900, and established its
seal of approval in 1909. Every recipe in this publication has been tested until perfect
for ease, reliability, and great taste by the Good Housekeeping Test Kitchen.

Hearst Communications, Inc. has made every effort to ensure that all information in this
publication is accurate. However, due to differing conditions, tools, and individual skills,
Hearst Communications, Inc. cannot be responsible for any injuries, losses, and/or
damages that may result from the use of any information in this publication.

Distributed in Canada by Sterling Publishing
c/o Canadian Manda Group, 664 Annette Street
Toronto, Ontario M6S 2C8, Canada
Distributed in Australia by NewSouth Books
University of New South Wales, Sydney, NSW 2052, Australia

For information about custom editions, special sales, and premium and corporate purchases,
please contact Sterling Special Sales at 800-805-5489 or specialsales@sterlingpublishing.com.

Manufactured in China

2 4 6 8 10 9 7 5 3 1

sterlingpublishing.com
goodhousekeeping.com

Cover design by David Ter-Avanesyan
Interior design by Sharon Jacobs
Photography credits on page 126

# Contents

LEMONY BRUSSELS
SPROUT SALAD
(PAGE 30)

# Foreword

Welcome to our first ever salad book!

Salad, these days—it's what for dinner, lunch, appetizers, and side dishes. Since the mid-1980s when bagged salad was first introduced, packaged greens and salad kits have become a 4-billion dollar business—and have helped reimagine the world of leafy greens. Add to that successful salad chains like Sweetgreen, Tender Greens, and Chop't, which cater to our desire for healthful fast food with plenty of options. Salad has become craveable center-of-the-plate food. And as we look to eat less meat and poultry, salads of every description are an easy way to go meatless.

If you think salad as dinner won't fly in your house, consider delicious options like Ginger Pork & Cucumber Salad, Kale & Roasted Cauliflower Salad, and Roasted Sweet Potato & Chicken Salad; try them and then customize to your fridge and pantry offerings. Consider flipping the green salad equation and start with a bed of grains, hearty chunks of toasted bread, or roasted veggie chunks. Add more vegetables (raw or roasted) for ballast, maybe some leftovers like rotisserie chicken, grilled tofu, steak, or cooked shrimp. Then include a few greens for texture and match a dressing (see our go-to list on page 26) to the family's favorite flavors.

Salad offers a world of infinite possibilities: From a humble bowl of greens to a full-blown main dish that incorporate protein, vegetables, greens, fruits, and nuts. When you're shopping, think seasonally. Winter squashes, cauliflower, broccoli, grains (served warm), apples, and pears in cooler weather. Stone fruits, asparagus, noodles (served chilled), tender greens, and berries for spring and summer. Check out our Switch It Up box on page 55. Play with the balance of sweet and savory ingredients as we do in Lemony Brussels Sprout Salad (page 30) and Thai Steak & Pear Salad (page 39).

For this book, we've developed salads for every occasion so whether you're hosting a barbecue, a fancy lunch, or making Tuesday dinner, you'll find a multitude of options. Looking for an American classic like a Cobb, or something with a bit of spice? We've got salad to satisfy everyone. Some require nothing more than chopping and shredding, for others you can fire up the grill, crank the oven, or heat a skillet. For ease, we've divided the book into four chapters: Leafy Greens, Protein-Packed Salads, Grain & Noodle Salads, and Side Salads.

Round out the meal with some warm bread, like tortillas, pita, baguette, focaccia, or flatbreads, and dinner is on the table!

SUSAN WESTMORELAND
Culinary Director, *Good Housekeeping*

KALE CAESAR PASTA SALAD
(PAGE 76)

# Introduction

Most salads start with greens, and knowing which green to use as the base can set you up for success.

Salad greens fall into two basic categories: delicate and tender, or assertive and slightly bitter. There are four basic types of lettuce:

**CRISPHEAD (ICEBERG)** varieties are crisp, mild-flavored, and stand up well to thicker dressings.

**BUTTERHEAD (BIBB, BOSTON)** is sweet-tasting and delicate and should be served with an appropriately light-bodied dressing.

**LOOSELEAF (OAK LEAF)** is tender but has a slightly stronger flavor than butterhead.

**LONG-LEAF (ROMAINE)** has long, firm, crisp leaves and is another candidate for rich, thick dressings.

For a well-balanced salad, combine strong-flavored greens like arugula and frisée with tender, sweeter lettuces like baby greens or mesclun. Bitter greens such as radicchio and Belgian endive also add colorful counterpoints to the salad palette.

> **TIP**
>
> We recommend rinsing and drying prewashed greens to refresh them and rinse off any bacteria from the surface of the leaves.

## GET THE MOST FROM YOUR GREENS

Greens are the base for most salads. From shopping to storing, follow these four simple steps for delicious salads every time.

**1. CHOOSE:** Greens should have no bruised, yellowing, or brown-tipped leaves. Heads such as iceberg, romaine, and leaf lettuces should feel heavy for their size. If buying bagged or boxed greens, avoid withered, dark, or moist leaves.

**2. WASH:** No one wants gritty greens! Separate the leaves from the head, submerge them in a sinkful (or in batches in a salad spinner bowl) of cold water, and gently agitate the greens to loosen any dirt. If the greens are very gritty, repeat the process. Lift the greens from the water, leaving the grit to sink to the bottom. With curly-leafed greens like spinach, arugula, and tender herbs, dirt often gets trapped in the crevices of the leaves. Wash these individually under room-temperature water (the slightly warmer temperature loosens dirt better than cold water), and, if necessary, give the greens a second washing.

**3. DRY:** Wet greens spoil faster, dilute the dressing, and make for a soggy salad. Dry salad greens thoroughly before using or storing. A salad spinner is an easy way to dry greens, but you can also pat them dry with clean kitchen towels.

**4. STORE:** Wrap the rinsed, dried greens in a clean kitchen towel (or in a few paper towels), place in a plastic bag (pressing out all the excess air), and store in the vegetable crisper of the fridge. Tender greens will keep for two to three days; iceberg and other sturdy lettuces will keep for up to a week.

MIXED GREEN & HERB
TOSS SALAD (PAGE 16)

# 1 | Leafy Greens

The basic leafy salad offers nearly infinite possibilities. From fresh summer greens to warm vegetable salads, there's something here for every season. These veggie-forward, flavor-packed recipes can serve as a healthy and easy lunch or dinner. Bright vegetables and fruits, like beets and watermelon, bring color and zest to these novel recipes.

# Bacon & Apple Farro Salad

Need to beef up your quick salad recipe? Throw in some bacon.

PREP: 20 MINUTES    TOTAL: 30 MINUTES

2 cups apple cider

1 cup quick-cooking farro

Kosher salt

4 slices bacon

8 ounces halloumi, sliced ⅓ inch thick

2 tablespoons red wine vinegar

Ground black pepper

½ small red onion, thinly sliced

1 large crisp red apple (such as Gala), cored and thinly sliced

1 cup red seedless grapes, halved

2 tablespoons extra-virgin olive oil

1 bunch arugula, thick stems discarded

**1.** In a medium saucepan, combine the cider, farro, and a pinch of salt and bring to a boil. Reduce heat and simmer, covered, until tender, about 10 minutes. Let stand 5 minutes, then fluff with a fork.

**2.** Meanwhile, cook the bacon in a large skillet on medium heat until crisp. Transfer to a paper-towel-lined plate; break into pieces when cool.

**3.** Discard all but 1 tablespoon of the bacon drippings and return the skillet to medium-high heat. Add the halloumi and cook until golden brown, 1 to 2 minutes per side. Transfer the halloumi to a cutting board and cut into ½-inch pieces.

**4.** In a large bowl, whisk together the vinegar and ½ teaspoon each salt and pepper. Add the onion and toss to coat; let sit 5 minutes. Add the apple and grapes and toss to combine. Add the farro, drizzle with olive oil, and toss to combine. Fold in the arugula and bacon and top with the halloumi.

**SERVES 4:** About 150 calories, 6g protein, 15g carbohydrates, 8g fat (4g saturated), 2g fiber, 265mg sodium.

# Green Goddess Carrot Salad

With a light buttermilk dressing, this colorful carrot
salad is the perfect start to any meal.

## SALAD

**1 pound slim baby carrots, trimmed
and cut lengthwise in half (or in quarters
if large)**

**1 tablespoon extra-virgin olive oil**

**½ teaspoon salt**

**1 cup Green Goddess Dressing
(recipe follows)**

**1 head Bibb lettuce, leaves separated
and torn**

## DRESSING

**¾ cup buttermilk**

**½ cup mayonnaise**

**⅓ cup plain Greek yogurt**

**4 anchovies, or 2 teaspoons anchovy paste**

**2 tablespoons fresh lemon juice**

**1 tablespoon Dijon mustard**

**1 small clove garlic**

**Pinch of sugar**

**¾ teaspoon salt**

**¼ teaspoon ground black pepper**

**½ cup loosely packed fresh parsley**

**¼ cup packed fresh basil**

**3 tablespoons fresh tarragon**

**2 tablespoons snipped fresh chives**

**1.** Preheat the oven to 425°F. On a large rimmed
baking sheet, toss the carrots with the olive oil
and salt. Roast until crisp-tender and edges
are slightly caramelized, 20 to 25 minutes; cool
completely.

**2.** Meanwhile, prepare the Green Goddess
Dressing: In a blender, puree the buttermilk,
mayonnaise, Greek yogurt, anchovies,
lemon juice, mustard, garlic, sugar, salt, and
pepper until smooth. Add the parsley, basil,
tarragon, and chives; pulse until the herbs are
finely chopped. Makes about 2 cups; can be
refrigerated up to 1 week.

**3.** To serve, arrange the carrots over the lettuce.
Drizzle with the dressing.

**SERVES 4:** About 200 calories, 4g protein,
13g carbohydrates, 15g fat (3g saturated),
4g fiber, 775mg sodium.

# Mixed Green & Herb Toss Salad

Sprinkle in some edible flowers for an elegant touch
when entertaining. See photo on page 10.

**TOTAL:** 10 MINUTES

6 cups mixed spring greens, such as
   Bibb, pea shoots, and mâche, torn

2 cups mixed herbs, such as tarragon,
   dill, mint, and chives, chopped

1 cup shelled edamame

¼ cup extra-virgin olive oil

1 tablespoon fresh lemon juice

2 teaspoons Dijon mustard

1 teaspoon honey

Kosher salt

Ground black pepper

1 small shallot, finely chopped

Soft-cooked eggs and edible flowers,
   for serving (optional)

**1.** In a large bowl, toss the greens and herbs.
Fold in the edamame.

**2.** In a bowl, whisk together the olive oil, lemon
juice, mustard, honey, and ¼ teaspoon each salt
and pepper; stir in the shallot.

**3.** Gently toss the salad with the dressing and
top with eggs and flowers, if desired.

**SERVES 6:** About 125 calories, 3g protein,
6g carbohydrates, 10g fat (1g saturated),
2g fiber, 180mg sodium.

---

**TIP**

Edible flowers add a pop of color to the plate
and are a nice touch when entertaining. They
can be found in specialty grocery stores.

# Tapas Salad

Trim an inch off the base of your romaine hearts
to release all the leaves at once.

TOTAL: 10 MINUTES

3 tablespoons extra-virgin olive oil

2 tablespoons sherry vinegar

1 clove garlic, crushed with a press

Kosher salt and ground black pepper,
   to taste

1 cup Manchego cheese, packed
   and shaved

4 ounces Spanish chorizo, cut lengthwise
   into quarters

½ cup roasted red peppers, chopped

2 hearts romaine lettuce, leaves separated

1 baguette, for serving (optional)

**1.** In a large bowl, whisk together the olive oil, vinegar, garlic, salt, and pepper. Add the Manchego, chorizo, and roasted peppers. Toss well.

**2.** Arrange the romaine hearts on a serving platter. Top with the cheese mixture. Serve with a baguette, if desired.

**SERVES 4:** About 305 calories, 11g protein, 5g carbohydrates, 26g fat (9g saturated), 2g fiber, 640mg sodium.

# Feta-Dill Greek Caesar

This grilled twist on a classic is perfect for summer barbecues.

**PREP:** 10 MINUTES   **TOTAL:** 15 MINUTES

4 ounces feta cheese

⅔ cup extra-virgin olive oil

⅓ cup nonfat plain Greek yogurt

3 tablespoons fresh lemon juice

1 clove garlic

¼ teaspoon salt

¼ teaspoon ground black pepper

¼ cup packed fresh dill, chopped

3 hearts romaine lettuce

¼ cup roasted sunflower seeds

**1.** Preheat the grill to medium.

**2.** In a blender or food processor, puree the feta, olive oil, yogurt, lemon juice, garlic, salt, and pepper. Transfer to a medium bowl; stir in the dill.

**3.** Cut the romaine hearts in half lengthwise; grill until charred in spots, about 2 minutes per side. Serve immediately, drizzled with the dressing and sprinkled with sunflower seeds.

**SERVES 6:** About 325 calories, 6g protein, 5g carbohydrates, 32g fat (7g saturated), 1g fiber, 265mg sodium.

# Kale & Roasted Cauliflower Salad

Roasted cauliflower and fresh kale come together in a salad recipe designed to keep your heart healthy and your belly full.

PREP: 10 MINUTES    TOTAL: 35 MINUTES

1 pound cauliflower florets

5 tablespoons extra-virgin olive oil

Salt

Ground black pepper

¼ cup fresh lemon juice

1 bunch kale, ribs removed, chopped

¼ small red onion, very thinly sliced

⅓ cup crumbled feta cheese

⅓ cup golden raisins

⅓ cup pine nuts

**1.** Preheat the oven to 450°F. On a large rimmed baking sheet, toss the cauliflower florets with 2 tablespoons olive oil and ⅛ teaspoon each salt and pepper. Roast until the stems are tender, about 25 minutes.

**2.** In a large bowl, whisk together the lemon juice, the remaining 3 tablespoons olive oil, and ½ teaspoon salt. Toss the kale with the dressing. Let stand at least 5 minutes.

**3.** To the kale, add the cooked cauliflower, onion, feta, golden raisins, and pine nuts. Toss until well combined.

**SERVES 4:** About 370 calories, 10g protein, 27g carbohydrates, 28g fat (5g saturated), 6g fiber, 475mg sodium.

# Beet, Mushroom & Avocado Salad

This super salad is loaded with antioxidants, fiber-filled vegetables, and healthy unsaturated fats (hello, avocado!).

**PREP:** 10 MINUTES    **TOTAL:** 30 MINUTES

4 medium portobello mushroom caps

Nonstick cooking spray

Salt

¼ cup fresh lemon juice

3 tablespoons extra-virgin olive oil

1 small shallot, finely chopped

Ground black pepper

5 ounces baby kale

8 ounces precooked beets, chopped

2 ripe avocados, thinly sliced

2 sheets matzo, crushed into bite-size pieces

**1.** Preheat the oven to 450°F. On a large rimmed baking sheet, spray the portobello mushroom caps with nonstick cooking spray and sprinkle with ½ teaspoon salt; roast until tender, about 20 minutes. Let cool, then thinly slice.

**2.** In a large bowl, whisk together the lemon juice, olive oil, shallot, and ¼ teaspoon each salt and pepper; toss half the dressing with the baby kale and beets and divide the mixture among 4 plates. Top with the avocados, matzo, and portobello slices. Serve the remaining dressing on the side.

**SERVES 4:** About 370 calories, 7g protein, 32g carbohydrates, 26g fat (4g saturated), 11g fiber, 490mg sodium.

# Crunchy Chickpea Kale Caesar

The crispy chickpeas in this Caesar
salad totally trump croutons.

**PREP: 10 MINUTES** **TOTAL: 35 MINUTES**

**2 (15-ounce) cans chickpeas, rinsed and drained**

**2 tablespoons extra-virgin olive oil**

**Kosher salt**

**Ground black pepper**

**½ cup mayonnaise**

**2 tablespoons fresh lemon juice**

**2 tablespoons finely grated Parmesan cheese**

**1 tablespoon Dijon mustard**

**2 cloves garlic, finely chopped**

**1 teaspoon anchovy paste**

**1 large bunch kale, tough stems and ribs removed, chopped**

**2 small red or yellow bell peppers, seeded and thinly sliced**

**1.** Preheat the oven to 425°F. Pat the chickpeas very dry with paper towels. On a rimmed baking sheet, toss the chickpeas with the olive oil, ¼ teaspoon salt, and ½ teaspoon pepper. Roast 30 minutes, shaking occasionally; let cool.

**2.** In a large bowl, whisk together the mayonnaise, lemon juice, Parmesan, mustard, garlic, anchovy paste, and ¼ teaspoon salt. Add the kale and bell peppers; toss to coat. Top the salad with the roasted chickpeas and serve.

**SERVES 4:** About 415 calories, 14g protein, 43g carbohydrates, 22g fat (3g saturated), 12g fiber, 870mg sodium.

---

**TIP**

To play with flavor when making the roasted chickpeas add a teaspoon of curry, chili, or 5-spice powder along with the salt and pepper and bake as directed. Or bake as directed, then toss with ingredients like honey, hot sauce, or Parmesan cheese and bake an additional 5 minutes.

# Salad in a Snap

Pair a quick salad with everything from pasta to pork chops, and dinner is served! It all starts with a simple vinaigrette.

## Basic Vinaigrette

In a small bowl, whisk together **3 tablespoons vinegar**, **½ teaspoon Dijon mustard**, and a **pinch each of salt and ground black pepper**, then slowly drizzle in ¼ **cup extra-virgin olive oil**, whisking until the mixture emulsifies. As provided here, change the flavor by using **different vinegars**, such as balsamic, sherry, or tarragon, or experiment with your own favorites.

## Baby Romaine with Fennel & Citrus

Toss together a **5-ounce bag of baby romaine**; **1 cup thinly sliced fennel**; **1 cup jarred citrus segments**, drained; ½ **cup chickpeas**, rinsed and drained; and **6 thinly sliced radishes**.

**Note:** Use lemon juice or a combination of lemon and lime juices instead of vinegar.

## Greek Salad with Feta & Olives

Toss together a **5-ounce bag of spring mix with herbs**; **1 cup grape tomatoes**; **1 English (seedless) cucumber**, cut into ½-inch chunks; and ½ **cup pitted Kalamata olives**. Top with ¼ **cup crumbled feta or goat cheese**.

**Note:** Use tarragon vinegar or white wine vinegar.

## Carrot Coleslaw with Dried Cherries & Almonds

Toss together a **10-ounce bag of shredded carrots**; **1 large red bell pepper**, seeded and cut into ¼-inch-wide strips; ½ **cup dried cherries**; and ½ **cup toasted slivered almonds**.

**Note:** Use seasoned rice vinegar and add a teaspoon of toasted sesame oil.

## Apple Coleslaw with Golden Raisins & Pecans

Toss together a **16-ounce bag of coleslaw mix**; **1 Granny Smith apple**, cored and cut into ½-inch chunks; ½ **cup golden raisins**; and ½ **cup chopped pecans**.

**Note:** Whisk in 1 tablespoon light mayonnaise.

## Spinach & Endive with Pears & Walnuts

Toss together a **6-ounce bag of baby spinach**; **2 heads Belgian endive**, sliced; **1 Bosc pear**, cored and thinly sliced; and ½ **cup toasted walnut pieces**.

**Note:** Use raspberry vinegar.

# Garden Greens & Pumpernickel Panzanella

Toasted bread, zesty dressing, and beautiful watermelon radishes take this green salad to another level. See photo on page 2.

~~~~~~~~~~~~~~~~~~~~~~~~~~~~~~~~~~~~~~~~~~~~~~~~~
**PREP: 25 MINUTES**   **TOTAL: 35 MINUTES**
~~~~~~~~~~~~~~~~~~~~~~~~~~~~~~~~~~~~~~~~~~~~~~~~~

1 pound asparagus, trimmed and cut into 1-inch lengths

1 bunch green onions, cut into 1-inch lengths

2 tablespoons plus 2 teaspoons extra-virgin olive oil

Salt

6 cups (¼-inch cubes) pumpernickel bread

2 tablespoons fresh lemon juice

1 tablespoon white wine vinegar

1 tablespoon spicy brown mustard

1 tablespoon prepared horseradish

¼ cup chopped fresh dill

4 cups arugula

½ bunch watermelon or regular radishes, trimmed and thinly sliced

**1.** Arrange 2 oven racks in the upper and lower thirds of the oven and preheat it to 450°F. On a large rimmed baking sheet, toss the asparagus, green onions, 2 teaspoons olive oil, and ¼ teaspoon salt; spread in a single layer. Bake on the lower rack until the vegetables are browned and tender, about 15 minutes. On another large rimmed baking sheet, arrange the bread cubes in a single layer. Bake on the upper rack until crisp and dry, 10 to 12 minutes, stirring once.

**2.** Meanwhile, in a large bowl, whisk together the remaining 2 tablespoons olive oil, lemon juice, vinegar, mustard, horseradish, and ½ teaspoon salt; stir in the dill.

**3.** Toss the bread cubes with the vinaigrette in the bowl; add the roasted vegetables, arugula, and radishes; toss until well combined.

---

**SERVES 6:** About 330 calories, 11g protein, 51g carbohydrates, 10g fat (1g saturated), 9g fiber, 870mg sodium.

**TIP**

The watermelon radish is an heirloom Chinese daikon radish. To serve raw, slice it thinly or use a Y-shaped peeler to shave it for salads. You can also pickle it, sauté it, or roast it. Cooking will bring out its sweetness but dull its showstopping, vibrant color.

# Crispy Beet & Mozzarella Salad

Roasted beets give this salad the
perfect amount of crunch.

PREP: 15 MINUTES   TOTAL: 45 MINUTES

**1½ pounds medium beets, scrubbed,
trimmed, and cut into ¼-inch-thick slices**

**3 tablespoons extra-virgin olive oil**

**Salt**

**1 English (seedless) cucumber, chopped**

**10 radishes, trimmed and thinly sliced**

**6 cups arugula**

**3 tablespoons red wine vinegar**

**Ground black pepper**

**8 ounces fresh mozzarella, torn**

**1.** Arrange 2 oven racks in the upper and lower thirds of the oven and preheat it to 450°F. In a medium bowl, toss the beets with 2 tablespoons olive oil and ¼ teaspoon salt; divide and arrange them in a single layer on each of 2 large rimmed baking sheets. Roast until golden brown and crisp, 20 to 25 minutes, switching racks halfway through. Let cool.

**2.** In a large bowl, toss the cooled beets with the cucumber, radishes, arugula, vinegar, the remaining 1 tablespoon olive oil, and ½ teaspoon each salt and pepper. Divide among serving plates; top with the mozzarella.

**SERVES 10:** About 130 calories, 5g protein, 6g carbohydrates, 10g fat (4g saturated), 2g fiber, 205mg sodium.

# Lemony Brussels Sprout Salad

Brussels sprouts shaved ultrathin are a great
alternative salad base. See photo on page 6.

**PREP:** 20 MINUTES    **TOTAL:** 25 MINUTES

¼ cup fresh lemon juice

3 tablespoons extra-virgin olive oil

Salt

Ground black pepper

1 pound Brussels sprouts, trimmed
and very thinly sliced

1 small head romaine lettuce, chopped

⅓ cup packed grated ricotta salata
or Pecorino cheese

⅔ cup dried cranberries or golden raisins

½ cup smoked almonds, chopped

**1.** In a large bowl, whisk together the lemon juice, olive oil, ½ teaspoon salt, and ¼ teaspoon pepper; add the Brussels sprouts and toss until well coated. Let stand at least 10 minutes or up to 2 hours.

**2.** When ready to serve, add the romaine, cheese, cranberries, and almonds to the large bowl; toss to combine.

**SERVES 8:** About 200 calories, 6g protein, 20g carbohydrates, 13g fat (2g saturated), 5g fiber, 310mg sodium.

> **TIP**
>
> If you have a really sharp knife, you can slice the Brussels sprouts by hand, but it's much easier to use an adjustable-blade slicer or a food processor (plus, it saves time!).

# Arugula-Kale Harvest Salad

Add autumn's bounty to greens for a seasonal salad
topped with a snazzy vinaigrette.

**TOTAL: 10 MINUTES**

## SALAD

**8 cups arugula**

**2 cups kale, tough stems and
ribs removed, chopped**

**1½ cups avocado, peeled and sliced**

**¾ cup thinly sliced carrots**

**¾ cup chopped cooked butternut squash**

**½ cup sliced apple**

**½ cup sliced bell pepper**

**2 ounces salami, chopped**

**1 cup croutons, for garnish**

## VINAIGRETTE

**¼ cup extra-virgin olive oil**

**1 tablespoon Dijon mustard**

**⅛ teaspoon sugar**

**½ teaspoon kosher salt**

**½ teaspoon freshly ground black pepper**

**3 tablespoons fresh lemon or lime juice**

**1 tablespoon vinegar (red wine, sherry,
champagne, cider, or white balsamic)**

**1 finely chopped small shallot, or
clove garlic, or green onion**

**1.** Make the Salad: In a large bowl, combine
the arugula, kale, avocado, carrots, butternut
squash, apple, bell pepper, and salami.

**2.** Make the Vinaigrette: In a small bowl, whisk
the olive oil, mustard, sugar, salt, and pepper
with the lemon juice, vinegar, and shallot. Makes
about ⅔ cup.

**3.** Add just enough vinaigrette to lightly coat the
salad and toss. Garnish with croutons.

**SERVES 6:** About 140 calories, 4g protein,
13g carbohydrates, 8g fat (2g saturated),
3g fiber, 305mg sodium.

> **TIP**
>
> Peppery arugula is also known as rugula
> or rocket. The baby version is mild; older,
> larger leaves have a more assertive flavor.
> The large leaves can also be very gritty, so
> rinse them thoroughly.

# Grilled Watermelon, Tomato & Feta Salad

Grilled watermelon brings bright color and balanced sweetness to this summer salad.

4 (½-inch-thick) slices watermelon

5 ounces mixed greens

2 large yellow or red tomatoes, each cut into 6 wedges

1 bunch small radishes, trimmed and halved

4 ounces feta cheese, crumbled

2 tablespoons balsamic vinegar

2 tablespoons extra-virgin olive oil

¼ teaspoon salt

**1.** Preheat the grill to medium.

**2.** Pat the watermelon slices dry with paper towels. Grill until marks appear, 3 to 4 minutes, turning over once halfway through. Remove the slices from the grill and let cool until able to touch. Using a medium star-shaped cookie cutter, cut 8 or 9 stars from the watermelon slices.

**3.** Arrange the mixed greens on a serving platter and top with the watermelon stars, tomatoes, radishes, and feta. Drizzle with the vinegar and olive oil; sprinkle with the salt.

---

**SERVES 4:** About 230 calories, 6g protein, 27g carbohydrates, 13g fat (5g saturated), 3g fiber, 447mg sodium.

CRISPY SESAME PORK SALAD
(PAGE 51)

# 2 | Protein-Packed Salads

These hunger-quenching salads feature a variety of proteins, including steak, pork, chicken, and seafood. There are simple recipes you can put together in 20 minutes for a weeknight meal along with showstopping salads that will impress your next dinner guests. From American classics to international flavors, there's something here to satisfy everyone. Fire up the grill, or turn on the oven, and get ready for delicious and healthy meals.

# Autumn Squash Salad

Make this dish on the weekend and double the recipe
for a delightful lunch throughout the week.

~~~~~~~~~~~~~~~~~~~~~~~~~~~~~~~~~~~~~~~~~~~~~~~~~~~~~~~
**PREP:** 10 MINUTES    **TOTAL:** 50 MINUTES
~~~~~~~~~~~~~~~~~~~~~~~~~~~~~~~~~~~~~~~~~~~~~~~~~~~~~~~

2 (20-ounce) containers chopped
  butternut squash

1 pound skinless, boneless chicken thighs

2 tablespoons olive oil

Salt

Ground black pepper

5 ounces mixed greens

3 tablespoons fresh lemon juice

4 ounces goat cheese, crumbled

**1.** Preheat the oven to 425°F. On 2 large rimmed baking sheets, toss the butternut squash and chicken thighs with the olive oil and ½ teaspoon each of salt and pepper. Bake until the squash is tender and the chicken is cooked, about 40 minutes or until cooked through (165°F). Chop the chicken into bite-size pieces.

**2.** In a bowl, toss the chicken with the squash, mixed greens, lemon juice, and goat cheese. Season with salt and pepper to taste.

---

**SERVES 4:** About 385 calories, 28g protein, 28g carbohydrates, 20g fat (7g saturated), 9g fiber, 555mg sodium.

# Thai Steak & Pear Salad

This flavor-packed dish with sweet pears and spicy
chiles takes only 30 minutes to throw together.

**PREP: 20 MINUTES    TOTAL: 30 MINUTES**

1¼ pounds boneless beef strip steak

Salt and ground black pepper

¼ cup fresh lime juice

1 tablespoon fish sauce

2 teaspoons sugar

1 teaspoon water

1 small Bartlett pear, cored and
    thinly sliced

2 green onions, thinly sliced on
    the diagonal

1 small fresh red chile, seeded and
    thinly sliced

5 ounces mixed greens

1 cup fresh cilantro

Chopped peanuts, for garnish (optional)

**1.** Trim the fat from the steak and season with
½ teaspoon each salt and pepper.

**2.** Heat a large cast-iron skillet on medium-
high heat. Add the steak and cook to desired
doneness, about 3 to 4 minutes per side for
medium-rare. Transfer the steak to a cutting
board and let rest for 10 minutes.

**3.** In a large bowl, combine the lime juice,
fish sauce, sugar, and water. Stir.

**4.** Add the pear, green onions, and chile to the
large bowl. Toss to combine. Fold in the mixed
greens and cilantro. Serve the salad topped with
the steak and sprinkle with chopped peanuts,
if desired.

**SERVES 4:** About 245 calories, 31g protein,
11g carbohydrates, 9g fat (4g saturated),
2g fiber, 615mg sodium.

# Grilled Steak Tortilla Salad

Serve a plate of your favorite taco fixin's. Steak strips, jalapeños, and cilantro are tossed together in this south-of-the-border creation.

**PREP:** 10 MINUTES    **TOTAL:** 20 MINUTES

1½ pounds skirt steak

1 teaspoon chili powder

Kosher salt

Ground black pepper

1½ pounds plum tomatoes, diced

2 green onions, sliced

1 jalapeño chile, seeded and thinly sliced

2 tablespoons fresh lime juice

1 bunch arugula, thick stems discarded

1 cup fresh cilantro

Charred flour tortillas, for serving

**1.** Preheat the broiler or grill to medium-high. Season the steak with chili powder and ½ teaspoon each salt and pepper. Cook to desired doneness, 3 to 4 minutes per side for medium-rare. Let rest for 10 minutes before slicing.

**2.** In a bowl, combine the tomatoes, green onions, jalapeño, lime juice, ½ teaspoon salt, and ¼ teaspoon pepper. Toss in the arugula and cilantro; fold in the steak slices.

**3.** Serve with charred flour tortillas.

**SERVES 4:** About 340 calories, 41g protein, 9g carbohydrates, 17g fat (6g saturated), 3g fiber, 595mg sodium.

**TIP**

To char flour tortillas, place them on the grill for 1 minute per side.

# Steak Salad with Charred Green Onions & Beets

*Sous vide* is French for "under vacuum," and hyperskilled chefs use the technique to cook meat or fish to perfection. In the Test Kitchen, our favorite device is the Joule.

**PREP: 15 MINUTES    TOTAL: 35 MINUTES**

1 (2-inch-thick) boneless beef top loin steak (1 pound)

1 tablespoon vegetable oil

½ bunch green onions, halved

¾ teaspoon flaky sea salt

5 ounces mixed greens

½ small head radicchio, leaves separated and torn

4 cooked beets, quartered

¼ cup red wine vinegar

1 tablespoon extra-virgin olive oil

¼ teaspoon ground black pepper

2 ounces blue cheese, crumbled

### TIP

Don't have a sous vide device? Seared or grilled steak is equally delicious in this recipe.

**1.** In an 8-quart saucepot, set up the sous vide device as the package directs. Add water and set the temperature on the device to 130°F. Place the steak in a gallon-size resealable plastic bag; seal tightly, pushing out any excess air. Place the bag in the hot water. Cook 2 hours. Remove the bag from the water. Remove the steak from the bag; pat dry.

**2.** In a 10-inch skillet, heat the vegetable oil on medium-high until very hot. Add the green onions; cook until lightly charred, about 2 minutes, turning. Add the steak to the skillet. Cook 2 minutes, turning frequently; remove the skillet from the heat so the green onions do not continue to cook. Transfer the steak to a cutting board and let rest for 10 minutes; sprinkle with ½ teaspoon flaky sea salt and thickly slice.

**3.** In a large bowl, toss together the greens, radicchio, beets, vinegar, olive oil, the remaining ¼ teaspoon flaky sea salt, and the pepper. Transfer to a platter. Top with the steak, green onions, and blue cheese.

**SERVES 4:** About 315 calories, 29g protein, 9g carbohydrates, 18g fat (6g saturated), 3g fiber, 735mg sodium.

# Summer Farro Salad with Grilled Steak

Topped with a colorful veggie medley, this steak, grain, and kale salad checks all the healthy boxes.

**PREP: 20 MINUTES   TOTAL: 35 MINUTES**

1 cup farro

2 medium red bell peppers, seeded and quartered

5 tablespoons olive oil

1½ pounds boneless beef top loin steak, thinly sliced

Salt

1½ cups corn kernels

4 cups kale leaves, ribs removed, chopped

¼ cup balsamic vinegar

¾ teaspoon ground black pepper

**1.** Preheat the grill to medium-high. Cook the farro according to the package directions.

**2.** Toss the bell peppers with 2 tablespoons olive oil. Season the sliced beef with ½ teaspoon salt. Grill the steak and peppers, covered, until the steak is cooked to the desired doneness and the peppers are charred, 2 to 4 minutes per side. Chop the peppers.

**3.** Toss the cooked farro with the peppers, corn, kale, vinegar, the remaining 3 tablespoons olive oil, ¾ teaspoon salt, and the pepper. Thinly slice the steak; serve over the farro.

**SERVES 6:** About 420 calories, 27g protein, 35g carbohydrates, 19g fat (5g saturated), 5g fiber, 540mg sodium.

# Gingery Steak & Corn Salad

Corn is the secret weapon in this killer salad. Make it during the summer when the crop is in season. See photo on page 72.

**TOTAL: 10 MINUTES**

### VINAIGRETTE

½ **cup toasted sesame oil**

½ **cup rice vinegar**

⅓ **cup Dijon mustard**

1 **teaspoon grated, peeled fresh ginger**

**Salt and ground black pepper, to taste**

### SALAD

1 **pound sirloin strip steak, grilled
to desired doneness**

5 **ounces baby kale**

½ **cucumber, thinly sliced**

2 **ears fresh corn, kernels cut from cobs**

**1.** Make the Ginger Dijon Vinaigrette: In a small jar, shake the sesame oil, vinegar, mustard, ginger, and salt and pepper until well mixed.

**2.** In a serving bowl, combine the steak, baby kale, cucumber, and corn. Drizzle the vinaigrette on top and toss.

**SERVES 4:** About 290 calories, 28g protein, 20g carbohydrates, 11g fat (2g saturated), 3g fiber, 157mg sodium.

> **TIP**
>
> If you prefer cooked corn to raw kernels, toss them into a dry skillet for a quick sauté before adding to the salad. This is also a great way to warm up leftover kernels.

# Balsamic Roasted Pork with Berry Salad

We've paired roasted pork loin with bright berries, licorice-flavored fennel, and baby spinach for a colorful and satisfying no-fuss meal.

**PREP: 25 MINUTES    TOTAL: 35 MINUTES**

4 tablespoons balsamic vinegar

2 tablespoons extra-virgin olive oil

3 teaspoons Dijon mustard

2 teaspoons packed fresh oregano leaves, finely chopped

2 bulbs fennel, cut into ¼-inch-thick slices

1 small red onion, thinly sliced

1 (1-pound) pork tenderloin

Salt

Freshly ground black pepper

1 pound strawberries, hulled and sliced

¼ cup packed fresh basil leaves, finely chopped

5 ounces baby spinach

½ pint blackberries

## TIP

This salad is packed with potassium-rich produce—including strawberries, blackberries, and baby spinach—which helps keep blood pressure in check. Bonus: The berries' vitamin C assists in warding off wrinkles.

**1.** Preheat the oven to 450°F.

**2.** In a large bowl, with a wire whisk, stir together 3 tablespoons balsamic vinegar, 1 tablespoon oil, 2 teaspoons mustard, and the oregano. Add the fennel, tossing until well coated. Arrange the fennel on outer edges of a large rimmed baking sheet. To the same bowl, add the onions, tossing until well coated. Arrange the onions in center of the pan. Add the pork to the same bowl and toss until coated; place the pork on top of the onions.

**3.** Sprinkle the pork and vegetables with ¼ teaspoon salt and ⅛ teaspoon pepper. Roast 18 to 22 minutes or until meat thermometer inserted in thickest part of pork registers 140°F.

**4.** While the pork roasts, add basil to a large bowl. In the same bowl, whisk together the remaining 1 tablespoon balsamic vinegar, 1 tablespoon oil, 1 teaspoon mustard, and ⅛ teaspoon salt until well combined. When the pork is fully cooked, remove the baking sheet from the oven and let meat stand for 5 minutes.

**5.** After 5 minutes, thinly slice the pork. Add the fennel, onion, spinach, and strawberries to the large bowl. Pour the dressing on top and toss until well combined. Divide the salad among 4 serving plates. Top with the blackberries and pork and serve.

**SERVES 4:** About 315 calories, 26g protein, 30g carbohydrates, 11g fat (2g saturated), 10g fiber, 480mg sodium.

# Ginger Pork & Cucumber Salad

Freshen up this spicy pork bowl with fresh mint and cilantro.
White rice acts as a neutral base for the heat in this dish.

**PREP:** 15 MINUTES    **TOTAL:** 30 MINUTES

1 tablespoon canola oil

1 pound ground pork

2 cloves garlic, finely chopped

1 small fresh red chile (seeded, if desired), finely chopped

2 tablespoons plus ½ tablespoon grated, peeled fresh ginger

4 tablespoons fresh lime juice

2 tablespoons low-sodium soy sauce

1 teaspoon light brown sugar

1 English (seedless) cucumber, thinly sliced

2 green onions, thinly sliced

1 cup fresh cilantro

½ cup fresh mint

1 cup cooked long-grain white rice, for serving

**1.** In a large cast-iron skillet, heat the canola oil on medium heat. Brown the pork, about 7 minutes. Stir in the garlic, chile, and 2 tablespoons ginger. Remove from the heat and toss with 2 tablespoons lime juice and 1 tablespoon soy sauce; add up to ¼ cup water if the mixture is too dry.

**2.** In a medium bowl, whisk together the remaining 2 tablespoons lime juice, 1 tablespoon soy sauce, ½ tablespoon ginger, and the brown sugar. Toss with the cucumber and green onions; fold in the cilantro and mint. Serve with the pork over the long-grain rice.

**SERVES 4:** About 475 calories, 26g protein, 44g carbohydrates, 23g fat (6g saturated), 3g fiber, 435mg sodium.

# Pork & Rice Noodle Salad

Mint and basil add pops of freshness to this hearty noodle bowl.

**PREP: 10 MINUTES    TOTAL: 25 MINUTES**

1 (1-pound) pork tenderloin

Salt

3 tablespoons fish sauce

3 tablespoons cider vinegar

2 cloves garlic, crushed with a press

8 ounces thin rice noodles, cooked as the label directs

1 cup shredded carrots

½ cup fresh basil

½ cup fresh mint

¼ cup finely chopped peanuts

**1.** Preheat the grill to medium.

**2.** Cut the pork tenderloin into 1-inch-thick medallions; season all over with ⅛ teaspoon salt. Grill until cooked to 145°F, 4 to 6 minutes, turning over once.

**3.** In a small bowl, whisk together the fish sauce, vinegar, and garlic. Toss half of the vinegar mixture with the rice noodles, shredded carrots, basil, and mint.

**4.** Chop the pork into bite-size pieces and serve over the rice noodle mixture. Drizzle with the remaining vinegar mixture. Top with peanuts.

**SERVES 4:** About 405 calories, 28g protein, 54g carbohydrates, 8g fat (2g saturated), 2g fiber, 1,035mg sodium.

# Crispy Sesame Pork Salad

For perfectly crisp meat, test the oil temperature before frying. Drop in a bread crumb; if it sizzles, it's hot enough. See photo on page 34.

TOTAL: 30 MINUTES

3 tablespoons low-sodium soy sauce

2 tablespoons light brown sugar

⅓ cup panko bread crumbs

2 tablespoons sesame seeds

1 large egg

4 thin boneless pork chops
  (about 1 pound total)

3 tablespoons canola oil

5 ounces mixed greens

1 cup grape tomatoes, halved

1 cup shredded carrots

**1.** In a small saucepan, whisk together the soy sauce and brown sugar. Heat to simmering on medium. Simmer for 2 minutes; set aside to cool.

**2.** On a medium plate, combine the panko and sesame seeds. In a shallow bowl, beat the egg. Dip each pork chop into the beaten egg, then coat it in the panko mixture.

**3.** In a 12-inch skillet, heat the oil on medium-high until hot. Fry the chops until cooked to 145°F, about 3 minutes per side. Drain on paper towels, then cut into cubes.

**4.** In a large bowl, toss the greens with the grape tomatoes, carrots, pork, and soy reduction.

---

**SERVES 4:** About 375 calories, 24g protein, 19g carbohydrates, 22g fat (4g saturated), 2g fiber, 520mg sodium.

# Rotisserie Chicken Cobb Salad

Top a classic salad with an already-cooked rotisserie chicken for a major time-saver.

**PREP:** 15 MINUTES    **TOTAL:** 20 MINUTES

**2 tablespoons extra-virgin olive oil**

**2 tablespoons red wine vinegar**

**Salt and ground black pepper**

**2 plum tomatoes, diced**

**1 rotisserie chicken**

**1 avocado, diced**

**4 slices bacon, cooked and broken into pieces**

**¼ cup crumbled blue cheese**

**4 thick slices iceberg lettuce**

**1 hard-cooked egg, grated**

**1.** In a large bowl, combine the olive oil and vinegar with ½ teaspoon each salt and pepper. Stir in the tomatoes.

**2.** From the rotisserie chicken, shred 3 cups meat; reserve the remaining chicken for another use. In a large bowl, combine the meat with the avocado, bacon, and blue cheese.

**3.** Serve the salad over the slices of iceberg lettuce and top with the grated hard-cooked egg.

**SERVES 4:** About 425 calories, 27g protein, 12g carbohydrates, 37g fat (9g saturated), 5g fiber, 955mg sodium.

**TIP**

Use the leftover rotisserie chicken in the Roasted Sweet Potato & Chicken Salad (page 56).

# Grilled Chicken Salad with Peppers and Avocado

You will never be in a salad rut again
with all the variations this salad has to offer.

TOTAL: 10 MINUTES

## DRESSING

3 tablespoons extra-virgin olive oil

1 tablespoon lemon juice

⅛ teaspoon salt

⅛ teaspoon ground black pepper

## SALAD

1 head or 2 hearts romaine lettuce,
   large leaves torn

1 pound chicken breast cutlets,
   grilled and sliced

1 red or yellow bell pepper, thinly sliced

½ English (seedless) cucumber, thinly sliced

1 avocado, thinly sliced

1 green onion, thinly sliced

¼ cup roasted almonds, coarsely chopped

¼ cup crumbled feta cheese

2 tablespoons dried cherries or cranberries

**1.** In a small bowl, whisk together the dressing
ingredients.

**2.** Divide the romaine lettuce among 4 large
plates and top with the remaining ingredients.
Drizzle with the dressing.

**SERVES 4:** About 370 calories, 28g protein,
15g carbohydrates, 25g fat (4g saturated), 7g fiber,
432mg sodium.

## SWITCH IT UP

**LETTUCES** Swap in thinly sliced kale,
baby spinach, arugula, or a lettuce mix.

**VEGGIES** Add 1 cup of raw sliced
cauliflower, broccoli, Brussels sprouts,
sugar snap peas, fennel, mushrooms,
tomatoes, celery, or shredded carrots.
Or try a cup of steamed asparagus,
artichoke hearts, or green beans.

**GRAINS** Add 1 cup of cooked grains or
roots: quinoa, farro, barley, lentils, beans,
sweet potatoes, chickpeas, edamame, or
winter squash.

**MEAT** Swap in 2 (5-ounce) cans tuna
packed in olive oil, 1 (14-ounce) can
salmon, 2 (4-ounce) cans sardines,
1 pound sliced grilled steak, or 12 ounces
cooked shrimp.

**NUTS** Swap in or combine almonds,
walnuts, pecans, hazelnuts, peanuts, or
pepitas.

**DRIED FRUIT** Swap in seasonal fruit such
as 1 large or 2 small sliced apples, pears,
mangoes, papayas, peaches, nectarines,
plums, or apricots; 1 cup blueberries,
raspberries, sliced strawberries, or
sliced figs.

**DRESSING** Swap in a flavorful vinegar
for the lemon juice: sherry, balsamic,
tarragon, or wine.

# Roasted Sweet Potato & Chicken Salad

Prepare the roasted sweet potatoes and miso dressing over the weekend for a delicious lunch all week long.

**PREP: 5 MINUTES   TOTAL: 30 MINUTES**

2½ pounds sweet potatoes, cut into ½-inch chunks

2 tablespoons extra-virgin olive oil

¼ teaspoon salt

¼ cup seasoned rice vinegar

2 tablespoons toasted sesame oil

1 tablespoon miso paste

1 tablespoon finely chopped, peeled fresh ginger

¼ teaspoon ground black pepper

20 ounces mixed greens

2 rotisserie chicken-breast halves (about 8 ounces total), sliced

1 avocado, sliced

Sesame seeds, for garnish

**1.** Preheat the oven to 450°F. On a large rimmed baking sheet, toss the sweet potatoes with the olive oil and salt; roast until tender, about 25 minutes.

**2.** In a small bowl, whisk together the vinegar, sesame oil, miso, ginger, and pepper.

**3.** Place 5 ounces of mixed greens on each of 4 plates; divide evenly and top each with the sweet potatoes, chicken, and avocado. Drizzle with the miso vinaigrette and top with sesame seeds.

**SERVES 4:** About 480 calories, 21g protein, 48g carbohydrates, 24g fat (4g saturated), 11g fiber, 990mg sodium.

# Sesame Chicken Slaw Mason Jar Salad

Layer up crunchy ingredients in a beloved portable container for a fresh take on lunch.

**TOTAL: 10 MINUTES**

- 2 tablespoons store-bought sesame-ginger dressing
- ½ cup chopped red cabbage
- ½ cup chopped cooked chicken
- ¼ cup shredded carrots
- ½ cup cooked quinoa
- 2 tablespoons dry-roasted edamame or wasabi peas

**1.** In a 16-ounce mason jar, layer the ingredients in the following order: dressing, cabbage, chicken, carrots, quinoa, and edamame. Screw on the lid and refrigerate until ready to eat.

**2.** When ready to eat, shake the jar until the contents are mixed. Enjoy.

**SERVES 1:** About 410 calories, 29g protein, 35g carbohydrates, 16g fat (3g saturated), 7g fiber, 402mg sodium.

### TIP

When building a mason jar salad, start with your dressing, add sturdy vegetables and proteins, and top with delicate foods like lettuce and cheese. Pop on the lid and set in your lunch bag. When you are ready to eat, just shake, grab a fork, and dig in.

# Chicken & Red Plum Salad

Chargrilled plums make this nutty salad
a summer standout.

PREP: 10 MINUTES    TOTAL: 20 MINUTES

4 (6-ounce) boneless, skinless
chicken breasts

2 tablespoons plus 1 teaspooon
extra-virgin olive oil

Salt and ground black pepper

4 red plums, cut into 1-inch wedges

2 green onions, thinly sliced

6 cups baby arugula

½ cup fresh dill, very roughly chopped

¼ cup roasted almonds, chopped

**1.** Preheat the grill to medium. Rub the chicken breasts with 1 teaspoon olive oil and season with salt and pepper. In a large bowl, toss the plums with 1 tablespoon olive oil and season with salt and pepper.

**2.** Grill the chicken until cooked through (165°F), 5 to 7 minutes per side. Transfer to a cutting board. Grill the plums until just charred, 2 to 3 minutes per side; return to the bowl and toss with the remaining 1 tablespoon olive oil and the green onions.

**3.** Slice the chicken and add it to the bowl (along with any juices); toss to combine. Fold in the arugula, dill, and roasted almonds.

**SERVES 4:** About 355 calories, 38g protein, 12g carbohydrates, 17g fat (3g saturated), 3g fiber, 345mg sodium.

# Caribbean Salmon & Mango Salad

With ingredients like coconut milk and chopped mango,
this island dinner is sure to fill you up.

**PREP:** 10 MINUTES    **TOTAL:** 20 MINUTES

1 (14-ounce) can coconut milk, shaken

2 cloves garlic, crushed with a press

¼ teaspoon ground black pepper

1 pound skinless, boneless salmon,
    cut into 1-inch cubes

½ teaspoon salt

3 cups cooked white rice

1 medium mango, finely chopped

3 cups arugula

¼ cup fresh dill, loosely packed

**1.** In a 10-inch skillet, heat the coconut milk, garlic, and pepper to simmering on medium. Season the salmon with the salt; add to the skillet. Cook until the salmon is done, about 5 minutes. Transfer the cooked salmon pieces to a plate and set aside. Discard the coconut mixture.

**2.** In a bowl, toss the rice with the mango, arugula, and dill. Serve the salmon on top of the rice mixture.

**SERVES 4:** About 475 calories, 30g protein, 49g carbohydrates, 18g fat (11g saturated), 2g fiber, 355mg sodium.

# Radicchio Salad with Roasted Fennel & Shrimp

Serve this flavorful, protein-packed salad on
a thick slice of toast for a hearty meal.

PREP: 15 MINUTES    TOTAL: 30 MINUTES

1 bulb fennel

1 red onion

1 tablespoon extra-virgin olive oil

Kosher salt

Ground black pepper

6 slices bacon

¾ pound medium (26- to 30-count)
   peeled and deveined shrimp

2 tablespoons balsamic vinegar

1½ tablespoons fresh lemon juice

1 teaspoon sugar

1 medium head radicchio (about 8 ounces),
   halved lengthwise, cored, and thinly sliced

1 cup fresh flat-leaf parsley

4 thick slices sourdough or country bread

Manchego cheese, for serving (optional)

**1.** Preheat the oven to 450°F.

**2.** Trim and thinly slice the fennel and onion,
place them on a large rimmed baking sheet,
and toss with the olive oil and ¼ teaspoon
each salt and pepper. Roast until tender,
10 to 12 minutes.

**3.** Meanwhile, in a large skillet, cook the bacon
on medium heat until crisp; transfer to paper
towels to drain. Let the bacon cool for a few
minutes, then break into pieces. Season the
shrimp with ¼ teaspoon each salt and pepper.

**4.** Discard all but 1 tablespoon bacon drippings.
Add the shrimp to the skillet and cook on
medium-high heat until opaque throughout,
2 to 3 minutes per side.

**5.** In a large bowl, whisk together the vinegar,
lemon juice, sugar, and ¼ teaspoon each salt
and pepper.

**6.** Toss the dressing with the radicchio, roasted
vegetables, cooked bacon, shrimp, and parsley.

**7.** Toast the bread. Serve the salad over the
toasts and top with shaved Manchego cheese,
if desired.

**SERVES 4:** About 440 calories, 24g protein,
41g carbohydrates, 21g fat (5g saturated),
5g fiber, 1,295mg sodium.

# Roasted Shrimp & Poblano Salad

Spicy salads always make for delicious dinners.

PREP: 10 MINUTES    TOTAL: 35 MINUTES

2 medium shallots, sliced

3 poblano peppers, seeded and sliced

1 tablespoon canola oil

2 teaspoons chili powder

1 pound large (16- to 20-count) peeled and deveined shrimp

4 radishes, sliced

3 tablespoons fresh lime juice

½ teaspoon salt

5 ounces mixed greens

1 avocado, sliced

1. Preheat the oven to 450°F.

2. On a rimmed baking sheet, toss the shallots and poblano peppers with the canola oil and chili powder. Roast for 20 minutes.

3. When the peppers have been in the oven for 20 minutes, add the shrimp to the baking sheet. Return to the oven and roast 5 minutes. Cool slightly.

4. To serve, combine the shrimp mixture with the radishes, lime juice, salt, and mixed greens. Top with sliced avocado.

---

SERVES 4: About 215 calories, 17g protein, 9g carbohydrates, 12g fat (2g saturated), 2g fiber, 940mg sodium.

**TIP**

If you are sensitive to heat, make sure to remove the seeds from the peppers before roasting them.

# Nicoise Salad

Make and shake this shallot vinaigrette in a mason jar. See photo on page 72.

**TOTAL: 10 MINUTES**

⅔ cup extra-virgin olive oil

¼ cup whole-grain mustard

¼ cup red wine vinegar

¼ cup fresh lemon juice

1 medium shallot, finely chopped

1 teaspoon sugar

Salt and ground black pepper,
   to taste

2 (5-ounce) cans oil-packed tuna

½ cup oil-cured olives

4 hard-cooked eggs, quartered

1 pint cherry tomatoes, halved

5 ounces mixed baby greens

**1.** Make the vinaigrette: In a mason jar, combine the olive oil, mustard, vinegar, lemon juice, shallot, sugar, and salt and pepper; shake.

**2.** Prepare the salad: In a serving bowl, combine the tuna, olives, eggs, tomatoes, and baby greens. Drizzle the vinaigrette over the top and toss.

**SERVES 4:** About 210 calories, 9g protein, 2g carbohydrates, 18g fat (2g saturated), 1g fiber, 729mg sodium.

# Summer Tuna Salad with Sweet Potatoes & Basil

Luxurious oil-packed tuna and robust black-eyed peas make this main dish extra hearty.

**PREP: 10 MINUTES    TOTAL: 25 MINUTES**

**3 sweet potatoes, thickly sliced**

**¼ cup water**

**2 tablespoons canola oil, plus more for brushing**

**Kosher salt**

**Ground black pepper**

**2 (15-ounce) cans black-eyed peas, rinsed and drained**

**2 (5-ounce) cans oil-packed tuna, drained**

**1 cup shredded carrots**

**¼ cup cider vinegar**

**¼ cup fresh basil, chopped**

**1.** Preheat the grill to medium-high.

**2.** In a microwave-safe container, combine the sweet potatoes and water and microwave, covered, on High for 8 minutes, then drain. Brush the potatoes with canola oil; sprinkle with salt and pepper. Grill 10 to 15 minutes, turning once. Cut into bite-size chunks.

**3.** In a large bowl, toss together the black-eyed peas, tuna, carrots, vinegar, basil, 2 tablespoons canola oil, and salt to taste. Fold in the potatoes.

**SERVES 1:** About 445 calories, 27g protein, 49g carbohydrates, 17g fat (2g saturated), 10g fiber, 750mg sodium.

**TIP**

When buying oil-packed tuna, make sure the label lists olive oil rather than soybean oil as it's more flavorful.

PARISIAN POTATO SALAD
(PAGE 86)

# 3 | Grain & Noodle Salads

Perfect for barbecues, easy lunches, and filling dinners, grain and noodle salads provide a multitude of options. These recipes elevate basic potato and pasta salads to a new level. Enjoy fresh takes on the classics, featuring tangy dressings and unique spices, alongside innovative dishes with ramen and couscous. Cold salads are a refreshing side on summer evenings, while warm dishes full of veggies and grains are perfect for cold nights.

# BLT Pasta Salad

Vine-ripened summertime cherry tomatoes are served
up in this light and fresh pasta salad.

~~~~~~~~~~~~~~~~~~~~~~~~~~~~~~~~~~~~~~~~~~~~~~~~~~~~~
**TOTAL: 20 MINUTES**
~~~~~~~~~~~~~~~~~~~~~~~~~~~~~~~~~~~~~~~~~~~~~~~~~~~~~

**1 pound pasta**

**1 red onion, sliced and sautéed**

**8 slices bacon, cooked and crumbled**

**1 pint cherry tomatoes, halved**

**2 cups baby arugula**

**1.** Cook the pasta according to the package
directions; drain.

**2.** Place the pasta in a serving bowl and then
mix in the onion, bacon, tomatoes,
and arugula.

---

**SERVES 4:** About 400 calories, 16g protein,
67g carbohydrates, 10g fat (3g saturated),
4g fiber, 328mg sodium.

## VARIATIONS

### Tabbouleh Salad

Cook **1 pound pasta** according to the package
directions; drain. Place the cooked pasta in
a large bowl. Add **1 pound tomatoes**, diced;
**1 lemon**, zested and juiced; ½ **English (seedless)
cucumber**, diced; **2 cups fresh parsley**, chopped;
**1 cup fresh mint**, chopped; and **5 tablespoons
extra-virgin olive oil**. Mix until well combined
and serve.

### Smoky Tapas Salad

Cook **1 pound pasta** according to the package
directions; drain. Place the cooked pasta in a
large bowl. Add a **1 (15-ounce) can cannellini
beans**, rinsed and drained; **1 (12-ounce) jar
roasted red peppers**, drained and chopped;
**6 ounces Spanish chorizo**, sliced; **¼ cup extra-
virgin olive oil**; and **2 tablespoons sherry
vinegar**. Mix until well combined and serve.

SWEET 'N' TANGY PASTA SALAD

GINGERY STEAK & CORN SALAD (page 46)

NICOISE SALAD (page 65)

# Sweet 'n' Tangy Pasta Salad

Amp up your barbecue with this next-level pasta salad.

TOTAL: 10 MINUTES

1 cup mayonnaise

½ cup balsamic vinegar

¼ cup extra-virgin olive oil

2 cloves garlic, crushed with a press

Salt and ground black pepper,
   to taste

1 pound rotini, cooked, drained,
   and slightly cooled

3 stalks celery, thinly sliced

3 carrots, shredded

1 red bell pepper, seeded and chopped

5 ounces arugula

2 (15-ounce) cans cannellini beans,
   rinsed and drained

**1.** In a small container, combine the mayonnaise, vinegar, olive oil, garlic, and salt and pepper. Close the container and shake until thoroughly mixed.

**2.** In a large bowl, combine the rotini, celery, carrots, bell pepper, arugula, and cannellini beans.

**3.** Add the dressing to the pasta mixture and toss to combine.

**SERVES 12:** About 290 calories, 11g protein, 46g carbohydrates, 8g fat (1g saturated), 9g fiber, 285mg sodium.

# Soba Noodle Salad with Spicy Cilantro Hummus

Creamy hummus is used as a velvety sauce in a whole new take on pasta salad.

**PREP: 30 MINUTES    TOTAL: 1 HOUR 30 MINUTES, PLUS SOAKING**

## HUMMUS

1 cup dried chickpeas

1 teaspoon baking soda

4 cloves garlic

6 tablespoons fresh lemon juice

¾ teaspoon salt

¾ teaspoon ground cumin

¾ cup tahini

⅓ cup water

1 cup packed fresh cilantro, finely chopped

¼ cup Sriracha hot sauce

## SALAD

¼ cup seasoned rice vinegar

2 tablespoons canola oil

1 tablespoon soy sauce

¼ teaspoon salt

8 ounces soba noodles, cooked as the label directs, drained

1 cup frozen shelled edamame, thawed

1 cup shredded red cabbage

½ cup roasted cashews, chopped

Sesame seeds

**1.** Make the Spicy Cilantro Hummus: In a 4-quart saucepan, place the chickpeas and baking soda; add enough cold water to cover by 2 inches. Let stand at room temperature overnight; drain (do not rinse) and return to the pot along with enough cold water to cover by 2 inches. Heat to boiling on high. Reduce the heat to medium; simmer until the chickpeas are soft and the skins have loosened, about 1 hour.

**2.** In a food processor or blender, pulse the garlic with the lemon juice, salt, and cumin until chopped. Add the tahini and water; pulse until smooth. Drain the cooked chickpeas and add them to the tahini mixture; process until smooth, stopping and stirring occasionally. Stir the cilantro and Sriracha into the mixture. Makes 3½ ounces.

**3.** Prepare the salad: Whisk together the hummus, vinegar, canola oil, soy sauce, and salt. Toss with the soba noodles, edamame, red cabbage, and cashews. Top with sesame seeds and serve.

**SERVES 6:** About 550 calories, 19g protein, 37g carbohydrates, 38g fat (5g saturated), 10g fiber, 94mg sodium.

**TIP**

No time to prepare homemade hummus? Use ½ cup of prepared hummus as a stand-in. Proceed by stirring in the cilantro and Sriracha.

# Kale Caesar Pasta Salad

Whip up this slimmer dinner salad in no time. This easy
dish is less than 500 calories. See photo on page 8.

**TOTAL: 25 MINUTES**

1 pound bowtie pasta

6 tablespoons light mayonnaise

⅓ cup grated Parmesan cheese

3 tablespoons fresh lemon juice

1 tablespoon Dijon mustard

1 tablespoon extra-virgin olive oil

1 clove garlic, crushed with a press

½ teaspoon salt

½ teaspoon ground black pepper

1 large bunch kale, stemmed and chopped

8 medium radishes, cut into quarters

**1.** Cook the pasta according to the package
directions.

**2.** Meanwhile, in a large bowl, whisk together the
mayonnaise, Parmesan, lemon juice, mustard,
olive oil, garlic, salt, and pepper. Add the kale,
tossing to combine.

**3.** Drain the pasta and, while still hot, add it to
the kale mixture; toss. Let cool slightly, stir in the
radishes, and serve.

**SERVES 6:** About 390 calories, 14g protein,
62g carbohydrates, 10g fat (2g saturated),
4g fiber, 435mg sodium.

# Grilled Veggie Couscous Salad

Have leftover grilled chicken? Toss it into this veggie-packed salad to make a main dish.

**PREP: 15 MINUTES    TOTAL: 30 MINUTES**

**2 medium red bell peppers, seeded and quartered**

**2 portobello mushroom caps**

**2 lemons, halved**

**5 tablespoons extra-virgin olive oil**

**Kosher salt**

**5 ounces arugula**

**4 ounces Pecorino cheese, grated**

**1 cup couscous, cooked as the package directs**

**Ground black pepper**

**TIP**

Cover the cut sides of the lemons with a paper towel before squeezing.

**1.** Preheat the grill to medium-high. Brush the bell peppers, portobello mushroom caps, and lemons with 2 tablespoons olive oil. Sprinkle with ½ teaspoon salt. Grill the mushrooms until tender, about 15 minutes, turning once. Grill the lemons, cut sides down, until charred, about 8 minutes. Grill the bell peppers until softened, about 6 minutes, turning once.

**2.** In a large bowl, combine the arugula, Pecorino, couscous, the remaining 3 tablespoons olive oil, and ¼ teaspoon each salt and pepper. Thinly slice the bell peppers and chop the mushrooms; add to the bowl. Squeeze the juice from the lemons into the bowl. Toss well.

**SERVES 4:** About 450 calories, 19g protein, 42g carbohydrates, 23g fat (7g saturated), 5g fiber, 920mg sodium.

MASON JAR PASTA SALAD

BURRITO "BOWL" SALAD

# Mason Jar Pasta Salad

You'll look forward to eating this lunchtime salad all morning long.

**TOTAL:** 10 MINUTES

2 tablespoons store-bought or homemade balsamic vinaigrette (page 26)

½ cup cooked pasta

¼ cup chopped cucumber

5 grape tomatoes, halved

¼ cup cannellini beans, rinsed and drained

½ cup baby spinach

Fresh basil leaves, to taste

**1.** In a 16-ounce mason jar, layer the ingredients in the following order: vinaigrette, pasta, cucumber, tomatoes, cannellini beans, spinach, and basil. Screw on the lid and refrigerate until ready to eat.

**2.** When ready to eat, shake the jar until the contents are well mixed.

**SERVES 1:** About 255 calories, 9g protein, 39g carbohydrates, 5g fat (0g saturated), 1g fiber, 452mg sodium.

### VARIATION

## Burrito "Bowl" Salad

In a 16-ounce mason jar, layer **2 tablespoons store-bought Southwestern ranch dressing**; ¼ **cup canned black beans**, rinsed and drained; ¼ **cup corn kernels**; ¼ **avocado**, chopped; ⅓ **cup cooked rice**; 1 **cup chopped romaine lettuce**; and **1 tablespoon shredded Cheddar cheese**. When ready to eat, shake the jar until the contents are well mixed.

# Honey-Lime Ramen Salad

This recipe will remind you of cold sesame noodles, only with a fresher taste.

8 ounces Chinese curly egg
   or ramen noodles

¼ cup tahini

3 tablespoons soy sauce

3 tablespoons fresh lime juice

1 tablespoon honey

2 cloves garlic, crushed with a press

1 large English (seedless) cucumber,
   chopped

1 pint grape tomatoes, halved

3 cups thinly sliced Napa or savoy cabbage

¼ cup finely chopped fresh cilantro

**1.** Cook the egg noodles according to the package directions. Meanwhile, in a large bowl, whisk together the tahini, soy sauce, lime juice, honey, and garlic until smooth. Add the cucumber, tomatoes, and cabbage; toss until well coated.

**2.** Drain the noodles and rinse with cold water. Drain once more, shaking off as much excess water as possible. Add to the large bowl with the vegetables, along with the cilantro. Toss until well combined. Serve immediately or refrigerate, covered, up to 1 day.

**SERVES 8:** About 180 calories, 7g protein, 28g carbohydrates, 5g fat (1g saturated), 3g fiber, 340mg sodium.

# Macaroni Chopped Salad

This classic loaded pasta salad is a serious crowd-pleaser.

**TOTAL: 10 MINUTES**

½ cup Cocktail Ketchup

½ cup mayonnaise

2 tablespoons cider vinegar

2 tablespoons Dijon mustard

½ teaspoon kosher salt

½ teaspoon ground black pepper

1 pound shell pasta, cooked and drained

4 hard-cooked eggs, chopped

2 stalks celery, chopped

¼ cup chopped fresh parsley

¼ cup chopped red onion

**1.** In a bowl, whisk together the Cocktail Ketchup, mayonnaise, vinegar, mustard, salt, and pepper.

**2.** Add the cooked pasta, eggs, celery, parsley, and onion and toss.

**SERVES 8:** About 410 calories, 10g protein, 43g carbohydrates, 38g fat (9g saturated), 3g fiber, 732mg sodium.

## Cocktail Ketchup

In a blender, puree **1 (28-ounce) can whole peeled tomatoes** until smooth. In a medium saucepan, heat **2 teaspoons canola oil** on medium heat. Add **1 small onion**, chopped, and **2 cloves garlic**, chopped, and cook 6 minutes, or until browned. Add **⅛ teaspoon ground cloves** and **¼ teaspoon ground black pepper**; cook 1 minute. Add **⅓ cup packed brown sugar**, **⅓ cup cider vinegar**, **3 tablespoons tomato paste**, **1 tablespoon soy sauce**, and the pureed tomatoes. Heat to boiling on high heat. Reduce the heat to medium-low; simmer 50 minutes, or until thickened, stirring occasionally. Cool slightly. In a blender, puree until smooth. Stir in **¼ cup bottled horseradish** and **2 tablespoons fresh lemon juice** and refrigerate until cold. Will keep in the fridge for 3 weeks.

# Peanutty Edamame & Noodle Salad

Shirataki noodles keep this seriously flavorful
stir-fry under 500 calories a serving.

**3 (8-ounce) bags shirataki noodles,
rinsed and drained**

**3 cups frozen shelled edamame**

**2 cups frozen corn kernels**

**½ cup creamy peanut butter**

**½ cup rice vinegar**

**1 tablespoon Sriracha hot sauce, plus
more for serving**

**2 tablespoons water**

**½ teaspoon salt**

**3 cups shredded carrots**

**1 pint grape tomatoes, halved**

**1 medium Granny Smith apple, cored,
quartered, and thinly sliced**

**½ cup fresh cilantro, chopped**

**1.** Heat a large saucepot of water to boiling on
high. Add the noodles, edamame, and corn;
boil 2 minutes. Drain, rinse, and set aside to
drain well.

**2.** In a large bowl, whisk together the peanut
butter, vinegar, Sriracha, water, and salt. Add the
carrots, tomatoes, apple, cilantro, and noodle
mixture. Toss until well coated. Serve with
additional Sriracha on the side.

**SERVES 4:** About 455 calories, 22g protein,
50g carbohydrates, 22g fat (3g saturated),
13g fiber, 540mg sodium.

**TIP**

Shirataki noodles are gluten-free,
cholesterol-free, and vegan yam-based
noodles that are used in Asian cuisine.
They are a great low-carb, high-fiber
alternative for starchy noodles and can be
found online or in specialty stores.

# Parisian Potato Salad

This creamy side dish incorporates the flavors of
Nicoise salad into every bite. See photo on page 68.

**PREP:** 20 MINUTES    **TOTAL:** 45 MINUTES

Salt

3 pounds Yukon Gold potatoes,
 peeled and cut into 1-inch chunks

¾ cup plain Greek yogurt

3 tablespoons extra-virgin olive oil

2 tablespoons whole-grain mustard

Ground black pepper

4 stalks celery, thinly sliced

½ cup cornichon pickles, drained and
 thinly sliced

½ small red onion, very thinly sliced

5 large hard-cooked eggs, coarsely chopped

¼ cup finely chopped fresh parsley

**1.** To a large saucepot of salted water, add the
potatoes. Partially cover; heat to boiling on high.
Reduce the heat to maintain a simmer. Cook
until the potatoes are tender, 12 to 15 minutes.
Drain well; let cool 10 minutes.

**2.** Meanwhile, in a large bowl, stir together the
Greek yogurt, olive oil, mustard, and 1 teaspoon
each salt and pepper. Add the cooled potatoes
to the dressing; toss until well coated.

**3.** Fold in the celery, pickles, and onion; gently
fold in the eggs and parsley. Serve immediately
or refrigerate, covered, up to 1 day.

**SERVES 8:** About 215 calories, 8g protein,
26g carbohydrates, 9g fat (3g saturated),
2g fiber, 410mg sodium.

# Creamy Potato Salad

A teaspoon of sugar gives our rich potato salad a dash of sweetness.

PREP: 20 MINUTES    TOTAL: 35 MINUTES

**3 pounds all-purpose potatoes (about 9 medium), peeled and cut into 1-inch chunks**

**Salt**

**½ cup mayonnaise**

**½ cup milk**

**2 tablespoons distilled white vinegar**

**1 teaspoon sugar**

**Ground black pepper**

**2 large stalks celery, thinly sliced**

**¼ cup finely chopped fresh parsley**

**2 tablespoons snipped fresh chives**

**1.** In a large saucepot, combine the potatoes, 1 tablespoon salt, and enough water to cover by 1 inch. Partially cover the pot; heat to boiling on high. Reduce the heat to maintain a simmer. Cook until the potatoes are tender, 12 to 15 minutes. Drain well.

**2.** Meanwhile, in a large bowl, whisk together the mayonnaise, milk, vinegar, sugar, 1 teaspoon salt, and ½ teaspoon pepper. Add half the dressing to the potatoes; let cool.

**3.** Add the celery and remaining dressing to the potatoes; toss until well coated. Fold in the parsley and chives. Serve immediately or refrigerate, covered, up to 4 hours.

---

**SERVES 10:** About 190 calories, 3g protein, 25g carbohydrates, 9g fat (2g saturated), 3g fiber, 390mg sodium.

TROPICAL RADICCHIO SLAW
(PAGE 93)

# 4 | Side Salads

A salad is the perfect way to round out a full, healthy meal. Slaws, vegetable dishes, and classic side salads are all great options for adding flavor and nutrients to a main course. Pair these recipes with a simple roasted chicken breast, a baked fish fillet, grilled steak, or any of your other favorite proteins for a simple but tasty dinner. From leafy greens like kale and arugula to vegetables like sweet potatoes and pickled carrots, there are options here to complement any meal.

# White Bean & Broccolini Salad

Honey mustard and red pepper flakes give this veggie salad a unique sweet and spicy flavor.

~~~~~~~~~~~~~~~~~~~~~~~~~~~~~~~~~~~~~~~~~~~~~~~~~

**TOTAL: 20 MINUTES**

~~~~~~~~~~~~~~~~~~~~~~~~~~~~~~~~~~~~~~~~~~~~~~~~~

Salt

1 pound broccolini (about 3 bunches), trimmed

3 tablespoons extra-virgin olive oil

1 teaspoon lemon zest

2 tablespoons fresh lemon juice

2 tablespoons honey mustard

½ teaspoon crushed red pepper flakes

Ground black pepper

2 tablespoons capers, drained and chopped

1 (15.5-ounce) can small white beans, rinsed
    and drained

**1.** In a large pot of salted boiling water, cook the broccolini until the stalks are crisp-tender, about 2 minutes. Drain and transfer to an ice bath to cool. Drain and pat dry, then cut the broccolini into large pieces.

**2.** In a large bowl, whisk together the olive oil, lemon zest and juice, honey mustard, red pepper flakes, and ¼ teaspoon each salt and pepper; stir in the capers. Add the broccolini and white beans and toss to coat.

---

**SERVES 6:** About 145 calories, 6g protein, 19g carbohydrates, 8g fat (1g saturated), 6g fiber, 375mg sodium.

> **TIP**
>
> An ice bath is an easy way to quickly stop the cooking process or safely cool food. To create one, fill a large bowl with ice and cold water. Place the container with your food in the ice bath.

HEIRLOOM TOMATO SALAD (page 104)

WHITE BEAN & BROCCOLINI SALAD

# Kale & Bean Salad

This bright and earthy salad perfectly balances out
a hearty main dish like Sweet Potato Cakes.

TOTAL: 5 MINUTES

¼ cup light mayonnaise

2 tablespoons fresh lime juice

1 tablespoon soy sauce

5 ounces baby kale

2 (14-ounce) cans no-salt-added
   black beans, rinsed and drained

2 cups frozen shelled edamame,
   thawed

Sweet Potato Cakes, for serving (optional)

**1.** In a large bowl, whisk together the mayonnaise, lime juice, and soy sauce.

**2.** Add the baby kale, black beans, and edamame; toss until coated. Serve with Sweet Potato Cakes, if desired.

---

**SERVES 4 (salad only):** About 345 calories, 19g protein, 48g carbohydrates, 6g fat (1g saturated), 9g fiber, 554mg sodium.

## Sweet Potato Cakes

Preheat the oven to 450°F. Spray a rimmed baking sheet with **nonstick cooking spray**. In a large bowl, toss together **3 sweet potatoes**, peeled and shredded; **2 green onions**, thinly sliced; and ¼ **teaspoon each salt and ground black pepper**. Use a ¼-cup measuring cup to scoop and pack the sweet potato mixture onto the prepared baking sheet, forming 12 mounds placed 2 inches apart. Flatten each one slightly. Spray the tops with nonstick cooking spray. Bake until the edges are browned, about 25 minutes. Let cool.

# Tropical Radicchio Slaw

Switch up mayo-based sides for this colorful fresh slaw made with chopped pineapple. See photo on page 88.

See photo on page 88.

PREP: 5 MINUTES    TOTAL: 15 MINUTES

2 medium heads radicchio, cut into quarters from top to bottom

2 tablespoons vegetable oil

2 cups finely chopped fresh pineapple

¼ cup packed fresh basil, chopped

2 tablespoons fresh orange juice

½ teaspoon kosher salt

½ teaspoon ground black pepper

**1.** Preheat the grill to medium.

**2.** Brush the cut sides of the radicchio wedges with vegetable oil. Grill, cut sides down, covered, for 8 minutes, turning once. Transfer to a cutting board; cool.

**3.** Slice the grilled radicchio very thinly. In a large bowl, toss the radicchio with the pineapple, basil, orange juice, salt, and pepper. Serve immediately or refrigerate, covered, up to 1 day.

**SERVES 12:** About 40 calories, 0g protein, 5g carbohydrates, 2g fat (0g saturated), 1g fiber, 85mg sodium.

## TIP

The best way to peel and core a pineapple is to lay the pineapple on its side. Using a serrated or sharp chef's knife, cut off the top and bottom of the fruit. Stand pineapple upright and cut peel down from top to bottom in 1 to 1½ inch strips, rotating the pineapple as you work. Try not to cut away too much fruit as you work. Cut the pineapple lengthwise in quarters. Cut away and discard the hard center core from each quarter. Cut fruit into spears or chunks.

# Radish & Fennel Panzanella

Pair this fresh side with a classic roast chicken
for a wholesome, balanced dinner.

PREP: 15 MINUTES   TOTAL: 20 MINUTES

**4 cups torn crusty bread**

**1 medium onion, thinly sliced**

**1 bunch radishes, trimmed and quartered**

**2 tablespoons olive oil**

**¼ cup fresh lemon juice**

**2 tablespoons Dijon mustard**

**Salt and ground black pepper**

**1 medium bulb fennel, trimmed, cored,
   and thinly sliced**

**4 cups arugula**

**1.** Preheat the oven to 425°F. On a large rimmed baking sheet, spread the bread in a single layer and bake until golden brown and crisp, 6 to 10 minutes; let cool.

**2.** Raise the oven temperature to 450°F. Place the onion slices and radish quarters on a 15½-by-10½ inch sheet pan and toss with the olive oil. Spread into a single layer. Roast until the edges are golden, 15 to 20 minutes, stirring once.

**3.** Meanwhile, in a large bowl, whisk together the lemon juice, mustard, and ¼ teaspoon each salt and pepper until smooth.

**4.** When ready to serve, add the roasted onion and radishes, fennel, arugula, and toasted bread to the large bowl; toss well.

**SERVES 6:** About 135 calories, 5g protein, 25g carbohydrates, 2g fat (1g saturated), 2g fiber, 445mg sodium.

# Broccolini-Radish Salad

Enjoy this salad with grilled steak for
a simple and hearty meal.

**2 bunches broccolini, trimmed**

**2 tablespoons extra-virgin olive oil**

**½ teaspoon kosher salt**

**2 tablespoons Dijon mustard**

**2 tablespoons fresh lemon juice**

**1 tablespoon maple syrup**

**5 radishes, thinly sliced**

**2 green onions, thinly sliced**

**1.** Preheat the grill to medium heat. Toss
the broccolini with 1 tablespoon olive oil
and ¼ teaspoon kosher salt. Grill, covered,
4 minutes, turning occasionally.

**2.** In a large bowl, whisk together the mustard,
lemon juice, the remaining 1 tablespoon olive oil,
the maple syrup, and the remaining ¼ teaspoon
salt. Toss the radishes, green onions, and grilled
broccolini with the dressing.

**SERVES 4:** About 95 calories, 1g protein,
8g carbohydrates, 7g fat (1g saturated),
2g fiber, 169mg sodium.

# Corn-off-the-Cob Salad

Have leftovers from a barbecue?
Grilled corn is the star of this crunchy side salad,
which can be served hot or cold.

**TOTAL: 15 MINUTES**

**3 tablespoons fresh lime juice**

**2 tablespoons Dijon mustard**

**½ teaspoon ground cumin**

**3 tablespoons extra-virgin olive oil**

**½ teaspoon kosher salt**

**6 large ears corn, grilled**

**1 pint multicolored grape tomatoes, halved**

**¼ cup chopped fresh cilantro**

**¼ cup chopped fresh mint**

In a large bowl, whisk together the lime juice, mustard, cumin, olive oil, and salt. Cut the corn kernels off the cobs; add to the dressing, along with the tomatoes, cilantro, and mint. Stir until combined and serve.

**SERVES 5:** About 270 calories, 6g protein, 40g carbohydrates, 13g fat (3g saturated), 5g fiber, 154mg sodium.

**TIP**

We've got a quick and safe way to remove kernels from the cob: use a Bundt® pan! Place the cob in the center of the pan and slice downward along the sides to remove the kernels. They will collect in the bottom of the pan, and you will have less of a mess.

# Orange-Basil Quinoa Salad

Quinoa is a gluten-free supergrain that's high
in protein and fiber. This easy-to-make dish is a fresh
and filling complement to any entrée.

**TOTAL: 10 MINUTES**

¼ **cup fresh basil, chopped**

3 **tablespoons fresh orange juice**

3 **tablespoons sherry vinegar**

2 **tablespoons extra-virgin olive oil**

¼ **teaspoon kosher salt**

¼ **teaspoon ground black pepper**

5 **cups cooked quinoa**

5 **cups packed mixed greens**

**Orange wedges, for serving (optional)**

**Wild Salmon Cakes, for serving**

In a large bowl, whisk together the basil, orange juice, vinegar, olive oil, salt, and pepper. Add the quinoa and mixed greens, tossing to combine. Serve with orange wedges, if desired, and Wild Salmon Cakes.

**SERVES 4 (salad only):** About 520 calories, 22g protein, 79g carbohydrates, 17g fat (2g saturated), 16g fiber, 322mg sodium.

## Wild Salmon Cakes

In a food processor, pulse **1 pound skinless, boneless wild salmon**, cut into small chunks; **2 green onions**, sliced; and ½ **teaspoon orange zest** until finely chopped. Form into 8 cakes; freeze 10 minutes. In a 12-inch nonstick skillet, heat **2 teaspoons extra-virgin olive oil** on medium. Season cakes with ¼ **teaspoon salt**; cook 4 minutes per side. Remove from pan and serve.

# Cucumber & Rice Salad

This simple side dish will pair with any protein
for a complete, hearty meal.

PREP: 15 MINUTES    TOTAL: 40 MINUTES

1½ cups long-grain white rice

⅓ cup fresh lime juice

¼ cup extra-virgin olive oil

¼ teaspoon ground cumin

¾ teaspoon salt

1 large English (seedless) cucumber, sliced

1 ripe avocado, chopped

½ cup packed fresh cilantro, chopped

**1.** Cook the rice according to the package directions; spread it on a large platter to cool completely.

**2.** In a large bowl, whisk together the lime juice, olive oil, cumin, and salt. Add the cucumber, avocado, cilantro, and cooked rice; toss to combine.

**SERVES 6:** About 335 calories, 5g protein, 45g carbohydrates, 15g fat (2g saturated), 4g fiber, 295mg sodium.

# White & Wild Rice Salad

Wild rice adds a chewy texture and nutty flavor to this mixed rice dish featuring fall-favorite ingredients like cranberries and pecans.

**PREP: 25 MIN   TOTAL: 1 HOUR 20 MINUTES, PLUS COOLING**

½ cup wild rice

Salt

¾ cup regular long-grain rice

⅓ cup dried cranberries or currants

2 tablespoons olive oil

2 tablespoons red wine vinegar

½ teaspoon freshly grated orange zest

¼ teaspoon ground black pepper

2 cups seedless red grapes, cut in half

2 stalks celery, thinly sliced

2 tablespoons chopped fresh parsley

½ cup pecans, toasted and coarsely chopped

**1.** Cook the wild rice as the label directs, using ½ teaspoon salt. Cook the white rice as the label directs, using ¼ teaspoon salt.

**2.** In a small bowl, combine the cranberries with just enough boiling water to cover; let stand 5 minutes to soften. Drain.

**3.** Meanwhile, prepare the dressing: In a large bowl and using a wire whisk, mix the oil, vinegar, orange zest, ¾ teaspoon salt, and the pepper until blended. Add the wild and white rice and cranberries; toss to coat. Let cool 30 minutes, tossing several times.

**4.** Add the grapes, celery, and parsley to the rice mixture; toss until thoroughly mixed and coated with dressing. Transfer to a serving bowl. Sprinkle with pecans.

**SERVES 8:** About 220 calories, 4g protein, 34g carbohydrate, 8g fat (1g saturated), 3g fiber, 450mg sodium.

# Lentil Spinach Salad

Keep it lean by serving this heart-healthy salad
with seared salmon for dinner.

**TOTAL: 10 MINUTES**

¼ cup fresh lemon juice

2 teaspoons Dijon mustard

2 tablespoons extra-virgin olive oil

¼ teaspoon salt

¼ teaspoon ground black pepper

1 teaspoon fresh thyme leaves

½ small red onion, finely chopped

1 (15-ounce) can lentils, rinsed and drained

1 small English (seedless) cucumber,
    cut into pieces

4 cups baby spinach

¼ cup fresh dill, very roughly chopped

**1.** In a large bowl, whisk together the lemon juice, mustard, olive oil, salt, and pepper; stir in the thyme.

**2.** Toss the dressing with the onion and lentils, then fold in the cucumber, spinach, and dill.

---

**SERVES 4:** About 200 calories, 10g protein, 26g carbohydrates, 8g fat (1g saturated), 9g fiber, 177mg sodium.

**TIP**

Fish, like salmon, is a great weeknight dinner option, as it doesn't need a lot of time to cook. If serving this dish with salmon, give yourself an extra 10 minutes to prepare the fish.

# Heirloom Tomato Salad

Take a bite out of summer with this light, refreshing side salad dressed in a sweet champagne vinaigrette. See photo on page 91.

See photo on page 91.

~~~~~~~~~~~~~~~~~~~~~~~~~~~~~~~~~~~~~~~~~~~~~~~~~~~~~~~~~~~~~~~~~~
**TOTAL: 15 MINUTES**
~~~~~~~~~~~~~~~~~~~~~~~~~~~~~~~~~~~~~~~~~~~~~~~~~~~~~~~~~~~~~~~~~~

¼ cup extra-virgin olive oil

2 tablespoons champagne vinegar

1 teaspoon honey

Salt

Ground black pepper

1 pint multicolored cherry or grape tomatoes, halved

2 tablespoons finely snipped fresh chives, plus more for garnish

1 pound heirloom tomatoes, some sliced and some cut into wedges

Small fresh basil leaves, for garnish

**1.** In a medium bowl, whisk together the olive oil, vinegar, honey, and ½ teaspoon each salt and pepper. Add the cherry tomatoes and chives and toss to combine.

**2.** Arrange the heirloom tomatoes on a plate and sprinkle with ¼ teaspoon each salt and pepper. Spoon the cherry tomato mixture on top and garnish with additional chives and basil leaves.

---

**SERVES 6:** About 105 calories, 1g protein, 6g carbohydrates, 10g fat (2g saturated), 1g fiber, 185mg sodium.

# Pickled Carrot Salad

Carrot ribbons add elegance to any main dish and are
easy to make with a Y-shaped vegetable peeler.

¼ cup rice vinegar

¼ cup light brown sugar

¼ teaspoon kosher salt

2 large carrots, peeled

1 small fresh red chile, seeded and very thinly
  sliced

¼ cup fresh mint, finely chopped

Vietnamese Caramel Pork, for serving
  (optional)

Cooked white rice, for serving (optional)

In a bowl, whisk together the vinegar, 1 teaspoon
brown sugar, and salt until dissolved. Working
over the bowl and using a vegetable peeler,
shave the carrots into the bowl in long ribbons.
Add the chile and let sit, 20 minutes, tossing
occasionally. Drain the liquid and fold in the
mint. Serve the salad with Vietnamese Caramel
Pork and cooked white rice, if desired.

---

**SERVES 4 (salad only):** About 43 calories, 1g protein,
9g carbohydrates, 0g fat (0g saturated), 1g fiber,
93mg sodium.

## Vietnamese Caramel Pork

Whisk together ½ **cup low-sodium chicken
broth**, ¼ **cup brown sugar**, and **1 tablespoon fish
sauce**. Season **1 pound pork tenderloin** (cut into
1½-inch chunks) with **salt** and **pepper**. In a large
skillet on high, add **1 tablespoon canola oil** and
brown the pork on all sides; transfer to a plate.
Add the broth mixture and simmer until slightly
thickened, 2 to 3 minutes. Toss with the pork to
coat and cook 1 minute.

# Green Papaya Salad

The taste of this light, fresh salad will
transport you to Thailand.

**TOTAL: 25 MINUTES**

1 fresh red Thai chile or serrano chile,
   seeded and thinly sliced

3 tablespoons rice vinegar

Salt

4 ounces green beans, trimmed and
   cut into 2-inch pieces

½ large green papaya, or 3 unripe mangoes

1 large carrot, peeled

1 cup bean sprouts

1 cup cherry tomatoes, halved

¼ cup fresh lime juice

2 tablespoons light brown sugar

1 tablespoon fish sauce

1 large clove garlic, crushed with a press

¼ cup small fresh basil leaves

Chopped roasted peanuts, for serving
   (optional)

**1.** In a small bowl, soak the chile in 2 tablespoons
vinegar for 15 minutes; drain.

**2.** In a pot of salted boiling water, cook the
green beans until crisp-tender, about 2 minutes.
Transfer to a bowl of ice water; once cool, drain
and pat dry.

**3.** Use a julienne peeler or food processor to
shred the papaya and carrot. Transfer to a large
bowl along with the bean sprouts, tomatoes, and
soaked chile.

**4.** In a small bowl, whisk together the lime juice,
brown sugar, fish sauce, garlic, and the remaining
1 tablespoon vinegar. Toss with the salad, then
fold in the basil. Serve topped with peanuts, if
desired.

**SERVES 6:** About 75 calories, 3g protein,
18g carbohydrates, 0g fat (0g saturated),
3g fiber, 225mg sodium.

**TIP**

*Som tum*, the Thai name for this dish, refers
to the sound the mortar and pestle makes
during its traditional prep.

# Warm Wild Mushroom & Lentil Salad

This earthy mushroom and lentil salad
pairs well with a glass of Pinot Noir.

**PREP:** 10 MINUTES  **TOTAL:** 25 MINUTES

**1 pound mixed wild mushrooms, cleaned, trimmed, and sliced**

**¼ cup extra-virgin olive oil**

**2 cloves garlic, crushed with a press**

**¼ teaspoon salt**

**12 ounces lentils, cooked as the package directs**

**1 cup fresh parsley**

**¼ small red onion, very thinly sliced**

**⅔ cup store-bought or homemade balsamic vinaigrette (page 26)**

**6 (¼-inch-thick) slices blue cheese, for serving**

**1.** Preheat the oven to 450°F. On a large rimmed baking sheet, toss the mushrooms with the olive oil, garlic, and salt. Roast until crisp, about 20 minutes.

**2.** Toss the cooked lentils with the mushrooms, parsley, onion, and balsamic vinaigrette. Top with blue cheese slices and serve.

**SERVES 6:** About 320 calories, 12g protein, 20g carbohydrates, 23g fat (6g saturated), 7g fiber, 725mg sodium.

# Herbed Roasted Veggie Salad

This satisfying salad is packed with nourishing vegetables
like Brussels sprouts, broccoli, and carrots.

PREP: 15 MINUTES    TOTAL: 35 MINUTES

1 pound broccoli florets

1 pound carrots, cut into 1-inch wedges

½ cup extra-virgin olive oil

Salt

1 pound Brussels sprouts, trimmed and halved

3 medium shallots, sliced

1 cup fresh cilantro, finely chopped

½ cup fresh mint, finely chopped

3 tablespoons fresh lemon juice

**1.** Preheat the oven to 450°F. On a large rimmed baking sheet, toss the broccoli, carrots, ¼ cup olive oil, and ¼ teaspoon salt; arrange in a single layer and roast 10 minutes.

**2.** On another large rimmed baking sheet, toss the Brussels sprouts, shallots, the remaining ¼ cup olive oil, and ¼ teaspoon salt. Arrange in a single layer and add to the oven with the other vegetables. Roast until all vegetables are tender and golden brown, about another 20 minutes, stirring once halfway through. (Vegetables can be roasted up to 1 day ahead. Cool slightly; cover and refrigerate.)

**3.** Meanwhile, in a small bowl, stir together the cilantro, mint, lemon juice, and ⅛ teaspoon salt.

**4.** Toss the vegetables with the herb dressing. Serve warm or at room temperature.

**SERVES 8:** About 190 calories, 4g protein, 15g carbohydrates, 14g fat (2g saturated), 6g fiber, 250mg sodium.

# Lemony Arugula Salad

Tart lemon and arugula come together for a side
salad that packs a flavorful punch.

**TOTAL:** 10 MINUTES

3 tablespoons fresh lemon juice

2 tablespoons extra-virgin olive oil

½ teaspoon honey

¼ teaspoon kosher salt

¼ teaspoon ground black pepper

4 cups wild arugula

2 cups pea shoots

1 green onion, thinly sliced into matchsticks

Shaved Parmesan cheese, for serving

In large bowl, whisk together the lemon juice,
olive oil, honey, salt, and pepper. Add the
arugula, pea shoots, and green onion; toss to
combine. Top with the shaved Parmesan.

**SERVES 4:** About 95 calories, 3g protein,
6g carbohydrates, 8g fat (2g saturated),
2g fiber, 170mg sodium.

**TIP**

This salad is a refreshing accompaniment
to breaded pork chops or chicken cutlets.

# "Succotash" Kale Salad

Fresh corn is available in supermarkets year-round, so
we're bringing this side back into the everyday
—with edamame, bacon, and kale added to the mix.

8 ounces bacon, chopped

3 tablespoons extra-virgin olive oil

1 large shallot, thinly sliced

12 ounces tomatoes, chopped

Salt

¼ cup sherry vinegar

2 tablespoons Dijon mustard

1 large bunch kale, tough stems and ribs
    removed, chopped

3 cups fresh or thawed frozen corn kernels

2 cups frozen shelled edamame, thawed

**1.** In a 12-inch skillet, cook the bacon on medium until it is crisp and the fat has rendered, 8 to 10 minutes, stirring occasionally. With a spoon, transfer the bacon to a paper-towel-lined plate. To the same skillet, add the olive oil and shallot. Cook until the shallot has softened, about 2 minutes. Add the tomatoes and ½ teaspoon salt. Cook until the tomatoes have softened, about 5 minutes, stirring occasionally.

**2.** To make the dressing, transfer the contents of the skillet to a blender. Add the vinegar and mustard; puree until smooth.

**3.** In a large bowl, toss the kale, corn, bacon, and edamame with enough dressing to coat; let stand 15 minutes. Serve the salad with the remaining dressing on the side.

**SERVES 12:** About 145 calories, 7g protein, 12g carbohydrates, 8g fat (2g saturated), 3g fiber, 215mg sodium.

# Cucumber Mint Salad

Kalamata olives are the trick to
this Greek specialty. *Opa!*

**TOTAL:** 10 MINUTES

½ **small red onion, thinly sliced**

½ **English (seedless) cucumber, very thinly
sliced**

¼ **cup pitted Kalamata olives, roughly chopped**

**1 tablespoon red wine vinegar**

**2 teaspoons extra-virgin olive oil**

**Crumbled feta cheese and fresh mint, for
serving**

In a bowl, toss the onion, cucumber, and olives
with the vinegar and olive oil. Top with the
crumbled feta and fresh mint.

**SERVES 4:** About 75 calories, 3g protein,
4g carbohydrates, 5g fat (2g saturated), 0g fiber,
161mg sodium.

> **TIP**
>
> Kalamata olives can range in color from
> deep tan to purple to black olives. They
> have a meaty texture and a slightly bitter
> flavor. Like extra-virgin olive oil, they
> deliver polyphenols, iron, calcium, vitamin
> A, and fiber.

# Gravlax Confetti Salad

This unique salad with gravlax makes gourmet simple.
Serve it at brunch as an alternative to the
expected bagels and cream cheese.

TOTAL: 10 MINUTES

1 (15-ounce) can cannellini beans, rinsed and drained

1 English (seeded) cucumber, chopped

2 medium tomatoes, chopped

⅓ cup store-bought gravlax, chopped

2 tablespoons fresh lemon juice

1 tablespoon extra-virgin olive oil

¾ teaspoon salt

½ teaspoon ground black pepper

In a large bowl, toss together the beans, cucumber, tomatoes, gravlax, lemon juice, olive oil, salt, and pepper until combined. Divide among 4 plates and serve.

**SERVES 4:** About 135 calories, 9g protein, 17g carbohydrates, 5g fat (1g saturated), 6g fiber, 1,067mg sodium.

**TIP**

Gravlax is a Nordic dish where raw salmon is cured in salt, sugar, dill, and other spices. You can buy prepared gravlax at the supermarket in the deli section.

# Sweet Potato Salad

This colorful salad pairs well with lean pork tenderloin.

PREP: 10 MINUTES    TOTAL: 20 MINUTES

1¼ pounds sweet potatoes, peeled and cut into ½-inch chunks

5 stalks celery, thinly sliced

2 medium shallots, thinly sliced

¼ cup light mayonnaise

1 tablespoon red wine vinegar

¼ cup fresh flat-leaf parsley, chopped

¼ teaspoon kosher salt

BBQ Pork Tenderloin, for serving (optional)

**1.** In a medium saucepot, cover the sweet potatoes with cold water by 1 inch. Partially cover and heat to boiling on high. Reduce the heat to a simmer and cook until the potatoes are very tender, about 12 minutes.

**2.** When the sweet potatoes are cooked, drain well; transfer to a large bowl along with the celery, shallots, mayonnaise, vinegar, parsley, and salt. Gently fold to combine.

**3.** Serve alongside sliced BBQ Pork Tenderloin, if desired.

**SERVES 4 (salad only):** About 175 calories, 3g protein, 34g carbohydrates, 3g fat (3g saturated), 5g fiber, 182mg sodium.

## BBQ Pork Tenderloin

Preheat the oven to 450°F. Line a large rimmed baking sheet with foil. In a medium bowl, whisk together **2 tablespoons tomato paste**; **1 tablespoon honey**; **3 garlic cloves, minced**; **1 teaspoon chili powder**; **1 tablespoon vegetable oil**; and **¼ teaspoon each salt and ground black pepper**. Add **1¼ pounds pork tenderloin** to the bowl and turn to coat. Place the pork on the prepared baking sheet. Roast until cooked through to 145°F, 25 to 30 minutes.

**TIP**

Need another side? Roasted Brussels sprouts round out this meal nicely.

# Summer Salad with Corn, Zucchini & Mint

Break out the grill for this fresh
and filling summer salad.

**PREP: 10 MINUTES**   **TOTAL: 25 MINUTES**

3 large ears corn, husked

¼ pound zucchini, sliced

½ tablespoon canola oil

1 teaspoon chili powder

Kosher salt

2 (15-ounce) cans chickpeas,
  rinsed and drained

½ cup packed fresh mint, chopped

3 tablespoons fresh lime juice

1 tablespoon extra-virgin olive oil

**1.** Preheat the grill to medium-high. Grill the corn until charred in spots, about 12 minutes, turning occasionally. Cut the corn kernels off the cobs.

**2.** Brush the zucchini with canola oil; sprinkle with chili powder and ½ teaspoon salt. Grill the zucchini 6 minutes, turning once. Chop the zucchini.

**3.** In a large bowl, toss the corn and zucchini with the chickpeas, mint, lime juice, olive oil, and salt to taste.

**SERVES 4:** About 260 calories, 10g protein,
37g carbohydrates, 9g fat (1g saturated),
8g fiber, 651mg sodium.

**TIP**

Grill up kabobs to pair with this salad for a one-stop dinner. Toss chicken or firm-fleshed fish like salmon or swordfish with some zest from your limes and salt and pepper. Add the kabobs to the grill while grilling the corn and zucchini.

# Cucumber, Roasted Beet & Pistachio Salad

This whimsical salad will bring some energetic color
to your table during the winter months.

PREP: 30 MINUTES    TOTAL: 1 HOUR

**3 pounds medium beets, trimmed, scrubbed, and very thinly sliced**

**3 tablespoons extra-virgin olive oil**

**Salt**

**1 large English (seedless) cucumber, thinly sliced**

**2 tablespoons sherry vinegar**

**1 tablespoon toasted sesame oil**

**¼ teaspoon ground black pepper**

**½ cup roasted salted pistachios, shelled and chopped**

**1.** Preheat the oven to 450°F. In a large bowl, toss the beets with the olive oil and ¼ teaspoon salt; divide the beets between 2 large rimmed baking sheets, spreading them out in single layers. Roast 30 minutes, or until tender, switching the pans between the racks halfway through. Let cool.

**2.** Meanwhile, in a medium bowl, toss the cucumber with ¼ teaspoon salt; transfer to a colander to drain.

**3.** Toss the cucumber with the vinegar, sesame oil, and pepper until well coated; fold in the beets. Transfer to a serving platter and top with the chopped pistachios.

**SERVES 8:** About 155 calories, 4g protein, 14g carbohydrates, 11g fat (1g saturated), 4g fiber, 270mg sodium.

# Index

Note: Page numbers in *italics* indicate photos separate from recipes.

# **Photography**

COVER: Mike Garten

BACK COVER: Danielle Occhiogrosso Daly

Danielle Occhiogrosso Daly: 13, 20, 23, 38, 41, 45, 48, 53, 59,
    71, 85, 102

Mike Garten: 2, 6, 8, 10, 14, 19, 24, 29, 32, 42, 57, 60, 63, 66, 68, 72,
    75, 78, 81, 82 (macaroni), 88, 91 (salad), 94, 96, 100, 107, 111
    (salad), 112, 115, 121, 122

iStock: Fatihhoca (background) 82

© Con Poulos: 118

Emily Kate Roemer: 34, 37, 108

Studio D: Chris Eckert 7

Shutterstock: Leszek Czerwonka 111 (background)

# Metric Conversion Charts

The recipes that appear in this cookbook use the standard United States method for measuring liquid and dry or solid ingredients (teaspoons, tablespoons, and cups). The information in these charts is provided to help cooks outside the US successfully use these recipes. All equivalents are approximate.

## METRIC EQUIVALENTS FOR DIFFERENT TYPES OF INGREDIENTS

| STANDARD CUP | FINE POWDER (e.g., flour) | GRAIN (e.g., rice) | GRANULAR (e.g., sugar) | LIQUID SOLIDS (e.g., butter) | LIQUID (e.g., milk) |
|---|---|---|---|---|---|
| ¾ | 105 g | 113 g | 143 g | 150 g | 180 ml |
| ⅔ | 93 g | 100 g | 125 g | 133 g | 160 ml |
| ½ | 70 g | 75 g | 95 g | 100 g | 120 ml |
| ⅓ | 47 g | 50 g | 63 g | 67 g | 80 ml |
| ¼ | 35 g | 38 g | 48 g | 50 g | 60 ml |
| ⅛ | 18 g | 19 g | 24 g | 25 g | 30 ml |

| | | | | | | |
|---|---|---|---|---|---|---|
| ¼ tsp | | = | | | | 1 ml |
| ½ tsp | | = | | | | 2 ml |
| 1 tsp | = | | | | | 5 ml |
| 3 tsp | = | 1 tbsp | = | ½ fl oz | = | 15 ml |
| | | 2 tbsp | = | ⅛ cup | = 1 fl oz = | 30 ml |
| | | 4 tbsp | = | ¼ cup | = 2 fl oz = | 60 ml |
| | | 5⅓ tbsp | = | ⅓ cup | = 3 fl oz = | 80 ml |
| | | 8 tbsp | = | ½ cup | = 4 fl oz = | 120 ml |
| | | 10⅔ tbsp | = | ⅔ cup | = 5 fl oz = | 160 ml |
| | | 12 tbsp | = | ¾ cup | = 6 fl oz = | 180 ml |
| | | 16 tbsp | = | 1 cup | = 8 fl oz = | 240 ml |
| | | 1 pt | = | 2 cups | = 16 fl oz = | 480 ml |
| | | 1 qt | = | 4 cups | = 32 fl oz = | 960 ml |
| | | | | | 33 fl oz = | 1000 ml = 1 L |

## USEFUL EQUIVALENTS FOR DRY INGREDIENTS BY WEIGHT

*(To convert ounces to grams, multiply the number of ounces by 30.)*

| | | | | |
|---|---|---|---|---|
| 1 oz | = | ¹⁄₁₆ lb | = | 30 g |
| 2 oz | = | ¼ lb | = | 120 g |
| 4 oz | = | ½ lb | = | 240 g |
| 8 oz | = | ¾ lb | = | 360 g |
| 16 oz | = | 1 lb | = | 480 g |

## USEFUL EQUIVALENTS LENGTH

*(To convert inches to centimeters, multiply the number of inches by 2.5.)*

| | | | | |
|---|---|---|---|---|
| 1 in | = | | | 2.5 cm |
| 6 in | = ½ ft | = | | 15 cm |
| 12 in | = 1 ft | = | | 30 cm |
| 36 in | = 3 ft | = 1 yd | = | 90 cm |
| 40 in | = | | | 100 cm = 1 m |

## USEFUL EQUIVALENTS FOR COOKING/OVEN TEMPERATURES

| | Fahrenheit | Celsius | Gas Mark |
|---|---|---|---|
| Freeze Water | 32°F | 0°C | |
| Room Temperature | 68°F | 20°C | |
| Boil Water | 212°F | 100°C | |
| Bake | 325°F | 160°C | 3 |
| | 350°F | 180°C | 4 |
| | 375°F | 190°C | 5 |
| | 400°F | 200°C | 6 |
| | 425°F | 220°C | 7 |
| | 450°F | 230°C | 8 |
| Broil | | | Grill |

## TESTED 'TIL PERFECT

Each and every recipe is developed in the Good Housekeeping Test Kitchen, where our team of culinary geniuses create, test, and continue to test recipes until they're perfect. (Even if we make the same dish ten times!)